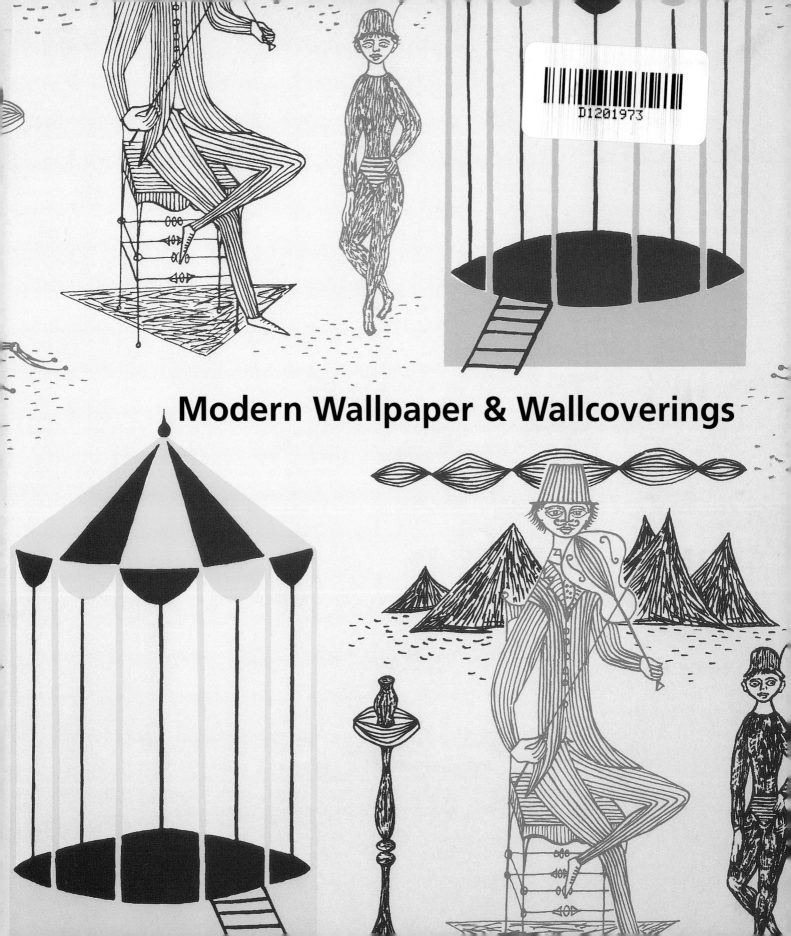

Modern Wallpaper & Wallcoverings

TO MY FATHER AND ANNE, WITH LOVE

First published in the United States of America in 2002
by UNIVERSE PUBLISHING
A Division of Rizzoli International Publications, Inc.
300 Park Avenue South
New York, NY 10010

02 03 04 / 10 9 8 7 6 5 4 1

Printed and bound in Dubai

ISBN: 0-7893-0689-1

Editorial Manager: **Judith More**
Art Director: **Penny Stock**
Executive Editor: **Zia Mattocks**
Designer: **Megan Smith**
Editors: **Lisa Dyer** and **Libby Willis**
Additional Text (Techniques): **Suzanne Ardley**
Picture Researcher: **Elena Goodinson**
Production Controller: **Janette Burgin**

Modern Wallpaper & Wallcoverings

INTRODUCING COLOR, PATTERN, &
TEXTURE INTO YOUR LIVING SPACE

Alice Whately

UNIVERSE

Introduction

FROM EAST TO WEST

The history of wallpaper in Europe began in the sixteenth century following the import of exquisitely painted panels by Chinese artists. Produced in sets and designed to give a continuous mural effect around the room – each panel linking with the next – early panels featured naturalistic motifs including flowers, shrubs, reeds, bamboo, birds and foliage on a plain background. After 1750 panelled papers became narrative in composition, showing large groups of people engaged in day-to-day activities such as farming, tea production, rice growing and porcelain manufacture. The popularity of Chinese wallpaper continued into the seventeenth century.

The quality and originality of Chinese designs meant that they outshone all others being produced in Europe at the time. In addition, other imports from the East including lacquer furniture and vases inspired the owners of the great houses of England to create Chinese rooms, with Oriental wallpaper providing the backdrop to the new exotic style.

In the second half of the eighteenth century, the trend for Chinese rooms began to fall from favour as print rooms became increasingly popular. Monochrome engravings were pasted on to walls, and were framed by engraved borders linked by paper swags, bows and other neo-classical adornments.

'Whatever you have in your rooms, think of your walls, for they are that which makes your house a home.'
WILLIAM MORRIS

The history of wallpaper in Europe owes much to French pioneers such as Jean Papillon, who invented continuous matching designs in1688, and his pupil Jacques Chavau, who printed the colours required using woodblocks. During the second half of the eighteenth century, Paris manufacturer Jean-Baptiste Réveillon introduced paper hangings designed by the leading decorative painters of the day. These papers took their inspiration from the classical motifs used by Renaissance artists to embellish wooden panelling, and included block-printed motifs of brightly coloured birds and beasts. The magnificent artistry of Réveillon's papers made them a popular American import, and examples can still be seen in New England houses today. Panoramic scenes, inspired by the Chinese concept of continuous pictorial decoration running around every wall in a room, were also produced in France – with companies such as Zuber and Dufour developing mural-like designs at the beginning of the nineteenth century. The panoramas were an instant hit in Europe and America but failed to appeal to the English market.

Wallpaper was first mass-produced in Britain in 1841 – with machine-printed designs taking over from block-printed ones. The new-look papers soon took over from fabric and wood panelling to become the main wall treatment in domestic interiors, although designs continued to simulate the look of pricier wall finishes, including striped and floral fabrics. As the nineteenth century progressed, patterns became denser and colours more brilliant thanks to the use of new chemical dyes in bright colours.

'Home is the wallpaper above the bed, the family dinner table ... the streets and squares and monuments and shops that constitute one's universe.'

HENRY ANATOLE GRUNWALD

Wallpaper also took hold in America during the eighteenth century. Wealthy homeowners ordered their papers from England and France, via agents who were commissioned to bustle back and forth with European samples, and ordered everything to match, from curtains to cushions. By the end of the Revolutionary War, demand was such that American wallpaper makers, often recent immigrants who had learned the secrets of flocking and hand-colouring in England or France, were able to set up workshops and advertise in local newspapers. By the beginning of the nineteenth century, Britain, France and America all had a thriving wallpaper industry.

PRODUCTION METHODS

BLOCK-PRINTING

The earliest Western wallpapers were block-printed, a process that involved individual designs being cut on blocks of seasoned hardwood. Paper was then fed in a continuous roll over a padded table and the blocks were dipped in a tray of colour before being lowered and pressed on to the paper's surface with a lever. The whole run of paper was printed with the first colour and then dried before the next colour was applied.

MACHINE-PRINTING

In the nineteenth century block-printing was superseded by machine-printing, a much less expensive method of production. As a result, wallpaper became available to the masses – as opposed to a privileged few. The first printing machine was patented by British textile printers Potters and Ross in 1839, and involved patterns being transferred to paper by means of copper rollers engraved with a raised design. The ability to print designs in several colours was developed soon after this initial invention. Each colour required a separate copper roller, and synthetic pigments like ultramarine blue and chrome yellow were used on rolls of continuous paper made from wood pulp.

FROM SHEETS TO ROLLS

The printing and hanging of decorated paper was conditioned by the fact that small sheets of paper were, for quite some time, universal. In English advertisements of the late seventeenth and early eighteenth century, however, paper hangings are offered for sale in pieces of 12 yards (11 metres) long and it is clear that sections were pasted together into convenient lengths.

In 1760 Founier of France produced long strips (in rolls) by pasting small sheets together. In 1798 Louis Robert, a workman employed in the mills of François Didot at Essônes, devised a method for making paper in continuous lengths, and patents were obtained in the following year. Although English patents to make paper 'without seam or join' were taken out in 1801, the use of continuous lengths was not allowed before 1830. The invention was in use in France, however, from 1810.

RELIEF PAPERS

Lincrusta (see page background) was developed in 1871 by Frederick Walton, the inventor of linoleum. Made of linseed oil, gum, resins and wood pulp spread over canvas, its surface was embossed with patterns produced by engraved metal rollers. Waterproof and durable, Lincrusta could be painted, stained or gilded to simulate traditional relief mouldings of wood, plaster and leather. A cheaper – and lighter – alternative, Anaglypta was invented in 1886 by Thomas Palmer. Made from cotton-fibre pulp, its relief patterns were created by hollow moulding.

During the nineteenth century both Lincrusta and Anaglypta were widely used for dados, providing a durable wallcovering for the area from the skirting board (baseboard) to the chair rail.

'A style does not go out of style as long as it adapts itself to its period.'
COCO CHANEL

TEXTILE EFFECTS

STAMPED LEATHER

Used to decorate walls as well as provide upholstery for furniture, embossed-leather coverings were taken to Spain by Moroccan Arabs long before wallpaper was invented. By the late seventeenth century, craftsmen in England and France were producing their own leather hangings, while wallpaper designers created less expensive imitation styles. The demand for leather-look wallpapers during the eighteenth century was intensified by the introduction of Japanese 'leather papers', which were imported into England and America after 1860.

FLOCK

Invented by the English in the seventeenth century, flock wallpaper was a cheaper alternative to the original fabric hangings. The pattern was printed or stencilled on to a sheet of paper with an adhesive before being strewn with 'flock' or powdered wool. The sheet was then gently pressed in order to allow the adhesive to take hold. When the superfluous flock was brushed away, a pile resembling velvet was left on the design. Flock wallpapers became less fashionable with the invention of colour printing in England in the middle of the eighteenth century, but enjoyed an unexpected revival in the mid-nineteenth century.

DAMASK

Often used for wallhangings, damask was created by varying the direction of threads in a single-colour weave. This labour-intensive procedure was also expensive and this added impetus to the invention

161
161

6/sheets
0146 X

162
162
13 Blocks Y6
10 Large Blocks
3 Small ones —
merge the small ones
broken no work on it
July 1911

162 A
3 Blocks. Y14
July 1911
had 18 proof shts
0295

163
6 Blocks. Y14
July 1911
0246

164
1 Block Y26
(for other colours
see after 145)
0244

289
241
166
155 X
159
154
217
288
311
313
315
316

of imitation wallpapers, which printed matt-finish motifs on to a smooth, polished ground. Although the elaborate designs of damask papers often echo those of flock papers, their smooth surface makes the overall effect less intrusive.

MOIRÉ

Moiré papers, which imitated the play of light on the natural iridescence of watermarked silk, were another popular substitute for the real thing. The subtle contrast between the matt and shiny areas of patterning in moiré papers offers more life than a flat painted wall, and at the same time supplies a wonderfully serene backdrop that does not interfere with the overall décor.

CHINTZ

In the seventeenth century the first multicoloured printed fabrics reached England via the East India trading company. With vivid colours and exotic patterns, the fabric, known as chintz, had a profound influence on Western designs. By the end of the eighteenth century, it was common for European wallpaper to feature the floral and figurative motifs – including hunting and battle scenes – that have become an integral feature of chintz-effect wallpaper ever since.

TOILE DE JOUY

In the eighteenth century, wallpaper designs known as toile de Jouy became available. Taking their cue from fabric wallhangings, which were printed using an engraved copper roller at a factory in Jouy-en-Josas, a little village south of Paris, the wallpapers featured narrative designs ranging from pastoral activities to scenes taken from classical mythology. Originally available in diluted shades of red, blue, brown or magenta on a neutral background, the inimitable appeal of toile de Jouy's finely drawn motifs endures to this day.

LEFT Taken from British artist and architect A W N Pugin's pattern book, these block-printed designs illustrate the flat stylized motifs of the formal Gothic style, on which his work was based.

INFLUENTIAL DESIGNERS

A W N PUGIN

When the British artist and architect A W N Pugin was asked to decorate the new Palace of Westminster during the1840s, he created dozens of block-printed designs all based on a formal Gothic style. Scornful of trompe l'oeil papers for giving what he viewed as dishonest illusions of depth, Pugin devised flat images inspired by heraldic emblems of stylized fruit and foliage forms as well as geometric designs taken from medieval tiles. These motifs were depicted in boldly repeating patterns and used a palette of rich dense colours, often in vibrant combinations.

BELOW An Arts and Crafts architect, C F A Voysey crossed disciplines to produce stylized wallpaper designs which derived from nature.

WILLIAM MORRIS

A founding father of the Arts and Crafts Movement in the mid-nineteenth century, William Morris aimed to make the best in handmade design available to the masses. Together with other devotees of the Movement – including the architect C F A Voysey – Morris crossed disciplines, designing furniture, textiles, stained glass and carpets. He was best known for his wallpapers, however, which he block-printed in order to escape the gaudy machine-produced designs popular at the time. As a result, his designs have a strongly organic quality: flowers flow and curve across the paper, while his gracefully intertwining leaves and stems effectively counter the tiresome effect of endlessly repeating motifs. Morris's influence gave wallpaper a new status. Not only did his approach inspire subsequent artists to view it as a credible medium for creative expression, but his designs, still produced commercially today, have also endured for more than 150 years.

CANDACE WHEELER

The influence of the Arts and Crafts Movement spread to America, inspiring designers such as Candace Wheeler to create her famous Honeybee wallpaper and frieze. A partner of Louis Comfort Tiffany in the late 1870s (their firm decorated the White House and Mark Twain's house, and won a number of prominent commissions in New York City), she entered the Honeybee design in the first American contest for an art wallpaper design in 1881. The contest was sponsored by New York wallpaper manufacturers Warren, Fuller & Company, which wanted to elevate American wallpapers to the high standards displayed by English companies at the Centennial Exhibition, held in 1876. Wheeler won a prize of $1,000 for this pattern. In 1883 she formed an all-women design firm called Associated Artists, and continued to produce wallpaper designs into the early twentieth century.

ABOVE American designer Candace Wheeler won a $1,000 prize for the delicate beauty of her Honeybee pattern, which she created circa 1880.

LEFT Designed in the 1860s, William Morris's boldly graphic Pomegranate wallpaper is manufactured by British company Sanderson, and is still in demand to this day.

TWENTIETH-CENTURY DESIGNS

1900–1940

The dawn of the twentieth century ushered in a dramatic shift in interior design. In place of the busily papered walls of high-Victorian style, the plain aesthetic of Arts and Crafts style provided the main influence. As the century progressed, wallpaper design took its inspiration from Art Nouveau – a style born out of the Arts and Crafts Movement but characterized by a much freer ethos. Organic motifs were based on the flowing asymmetrical curves of flowers and plants, although their superstylized form often made them hard to recognize. Long-stemmed lilies and poppies were the most popular motifs.

During the interwar years the Art Deco style predominated, with an aesthetic signature reflecting a variety of influences. Deco's geometric forms – circles, ovals, octagons, triangles and zigzags – were inspired by Aztec and Native American cultures, while papers depicting overlapping squares or oblongs derived from contemporary Cubist paintings. Wallpapers patterned with Egyptian motifs had first appeared during the last quarter of the nineteenth century as the British Empire consolidated its rule over Egypt. During the first half of the twentieth century Egyptian motifs such as scarabs, sphinxes, palm trees and camels enjoyed a revival and were frequently used in Art Deco schemes.

Naturalistic motifs in the Art Deco period included lush images of roses, dahlias and daisies. Often presented in baskets, festoons or garlands, their round heads were stylized and their densely packed images strongly outlined. Typical Deco colours included soft neutrals such as cream and grey, and bolder pastels such as peach, eau de nil and mauve. These were punctuated with stronger colours including orange, red, yellow, green and black. Visual contrast was further consolidated through the juxtaposition of the main wallpaper and a decorative border, which usually ran along the top or middle of the wall at dado or picture-rail level.

In addition to a renaissance of striped papers, the 1930s also witnessed the arrival of Bauhaus papers, which featured shimmering vertical, horizontal or wavy lines, or delicate latticework in pastel hues.

Launched in 1947, vinyl wallpapers consisted of a coat of polyvinyl chloride (PVC) bonded to a patterned or plain paper backing. Their appeal was durability, washability and a resistance to yellowing with age.

1950S

Valued for its rich variety of innovative designs, the 1950s produced wallpapers with abstract or stylized motifs, known as 'Contemporary' style. During this

BELOW Designed in 1901 by Koloman Moser, the organic curves and stylized appearance of this wallpaper is typical of early Art Nouveau style.

patterned areas within an interior was a key design element in the 1950s. As a result, wallpaper books were compiled in order to show how two contrasting wallpapers printed with patterns on a different scale but in the same colourway could be used on adjacent walls to complement each other. The contrast might be between walls within a room, rooms within a house, or the patterns on different types of surfaces such as walls and soft furnishings. This was an excellent decorating technique as, used strategically, it illustrated how wallpapers could be exploited to create changes of atmosphere within an interior.

LEFT Created in the mid-1950s, this paper shows the nipped-in waists and midi skirts of Christian Dior's famous New Look.

BELOW Piero Fornasetti's montage-style wallpaper, which he designed in 1950, reflects his humour and zany imagination.

decade the link between wallpaper patterns and the designs employed in contemporary fine art – which first made itself evident in papers created in the early twentieth century – was further consolidated by the work of British designer Lucienne Day, whose wallpapers featured linear patterns and ovoid shapes inspired by the work of abstract artists such as Henri Matisse, Joan Miró and Pablo Picasso.

More whimsical designs included the witty creations of American designers Ben Rose and Saul Steinberg. Kitchen wallpapers developed their own vocabulary, featuring brightly coloured fruit and vegetable motifs, which today appear delightfully kitsch but were then viewed as nothing more than light-hearted and cheerful. The trend, which was initiated in America, soon spread to Britain.

Bright colours were embraced as a reaction against the drab war years. A greater number of colours were combined to give variety, while textural contrast was created by juxtaposing patterned wallpapers with rough stone walls. The interplay between plain and

1960S

Everything about design in the 1960s was fresh and punchy, with clean graphic shapes, curved edges and pure bright hues dominating. Typical wallpaper motifs included sunbursts, giant circles and flying-saucer shapes, while kitchenalia papers featured recipes and bottles of foreign wine, which reflected the substantial increase in leisure travel at the time. Plant forms were another popular motif during the 1960s, especially in America and Scandinavia, where many designers were preoccupied with bringing the outside in.

Stylized flowers and leaves, originally inspired by Art Nouveau designs, were reinterpreted through the use of a bold bright palette, which grew increasingly lurid as the drug-induced psychedelia of the hippie movement gathered pace towards the end of the decade.

The general preoccupation with natural plant forms and phenomena was further evident in designs based on cobwebs and rainfall, while printed replicas of the figuring and grain of various species

OPPOSITE Verner Panton's injection-moulded plastic wall panels are a brilliant example of the punchy design of the 1960s.

RIGHT This wallpaper, which was designed by June Lyon in 1953, depicts television aerials and commemorates one of the most popular inventions of all time.

BELOW The juxtaposition of patterned wallpaper with walls covered in natural materials such as wicker, stone or wood was a popular decorating technique in the 1950s.

of wood were also fashionable. In addition, thanks to technical advances, microphotographic views of the molecular structure of substances such as myoglobin and insulin provided inspiration for a raft of funky abstracted designs.

The 1960s also saw the birth of Pop Art, which sought to narrow the gap between fine and commercial art and make it more accessible to the general public. As a result, influential figures such as Andy Warhol appropriated everyday items – most famously Campbell's Soup cans and Coca-Cola bottles – to screen-print their endlessly repeating image in varying colourways. Repetitive portraits of Chairman Mao, Marilyn Monroe and Elvis Presley followed, and paved the way for Warhol's famous Cows wallpaper, which featured a pink cow's head printed in a diagonal direction on an acid-yellow background.

1970S

Inspired by disco fever, the wallpapers of the 1970s reflected the dark surfaces, flashing lights and glitterballs of groovy nightclubs. Typical designs featured plant forms in muted or incandescent colours on shiny or dull metallic backgrounds – a look that made them perfectly suited to what *Vogue* magazine described as 'a Nickelodeon land of Art Deco with potted palms and mirrored halls'.

Since the 1970s, metallic finishes have also served as patterns in their own right. Most show random mottling across their surface that replicates the appearance of tarnished metals such as copper and bronze. What is more, these fabulous papers seem to change appearance according to the way light plays upon the surface, enabling them to provide a far more versatile wall decoration than ordinary plain paper. For example, areas of the wall where light hits the surface will sparkle brightly, while other areas not touched by direct light will appear more muted and mysterious.

Wallpaper in the 1970s also included stylized floral designs in pyschedelic shades – a hangover from the late 1960s when Flower Power was at its height. Other designs included heavily patterned prints such as bold geometrics and loopy ovals, which were rendered in fashionable shades of bitter-chocolate brown, deep purple and zesty tangerine. Moreover, patterns and colours were mixed and matched to create a satisfyingly scary clash; picking out one or two walls in a contrasting colour or design, or even covering a huge area of wall with a startling hand-painted supergraphic, were quintessential 1970s touches.

1980S

Wallpapers that reproduced the appearance of decorative paint effects were particularly popular in the 1980s as homeowners strove to break free from the intrusive designs of the previous decade.

Imitations of colourwashing, ragging, sponging and stippling – known as 'broken-colour techniques' – displayed, to varying degrees, gradations of pattern and tone, while pastel colours such as peach, mint, powder blue and violet predominated. Designs simulating limed wood were also popular, as were pale marble-effect papers.

Coordinated furnishings constituted another key feature of 1980s style. This was largely owing to designers such as Laura Ashley, whose matching papers and fabrics became ubiquitous in homes across Britain and America throughout the late 1970s and early 1980s. Mainly featuring floral prints – from itsy-bitsy sprigs to stylized cartouches of roses in antique shades – they also incorporated delicate shells, Regency-era stripes, bows, ribbons, trelliswork and kitchen vegetables. Each paper came with a complementary border, which sadly tipped the scales, making Ashley's fundamentally attractive and simple designs suddenly appear fussy and overdone.

The 1980s also threw up a number of fairly crude wallpaper designs. Patterns depicting abstract doodles, graffiti prints, hearts and nautical motifs were significantly lacking in subtlety, while a palette featuring scarlet, royal blue, navy, emerald green and gold compounded the garish effect.

1990S–PRESENT DAY

In response to the excessive design of 1980s interiors, the 1990s championed a back-to-basics approach. This was allied with recession as well as an increasing awareness of environmental issues. Staying in was the new going out, and our homes

RIGHT Op Art wallpaper, teamed with a Moroccan lantern, shag-pile rug and Indian silk cushions, creates a quintessential 1970s interior.

FAR RIGHT This soft-focus wallpaper depicting fey-looking girls with floppy hats and smocked dresses is sweetly reminiscent of 1970s style.

were viewed as healing havens – places where we could retreat in order to rejuvenate body and soul. Minimalism and eco-chic were the bywords for interior style, and texture was a key feature. As a result, natural wallcoverings, last seen in the 1960s, were big news – with designs in raffia, hemp, grasscloth and jute all experiencing a huge resurgence in popularity.

Environmental concerns are also addressed by Francesco Simeti, whose Acorn wallpaper was designed and digitally printed in 2000. Acorn paper is accompanied by wall text that explains the artist's intention: 'Set in the eighteenth-century format of print-room wallpaper, Acorn paper comments on environmental abuse with images from contemporary newspapers.' Using wallpaper as background, Simeti illustrates that our bucolic perception of the landscape may be in jeopardy. This powerful visual image of masked human beings dealing with a polluted environment filled with toxic waste and landfills harbouring poisons as yet undiscovered is an indictment of a society governed by consumption, with side effects that are affecting the land and all natural existence – including human.

REFLECTING THE TIMES

By the mid-nineteenth century current events had become commonplace as images on wallpapers, reflecting the tastes of the new middle-class market who could afford machine-printed designs. Images ranged from Gallipoli under siege during the Crimean War (1835–56) to the Prince of Wales's visit to India in 1921–2 as part of his world tour. The fashion for current-events wallpaper continued well into the twentieth century, eventually tailing off during the 1960s.

Examples of early commemorative designs include aeronautical images, which illustrate the huge advances in controlled powered flight, from the wood-and-glue constructions available at the turn of the century to the metal monoplanes that dotted the skies from the 1930s onwards.

Depictions of changing women's fashions were also popular. An exquisite example is the wallpaper commemorating Christian Dior's New Look collection, which was launched in 1947 and signalled an end to postwar austerity. Images of women wearing hour-glass jackets and long flowing skirts made with yard upon decadent yard of material reflected the full-on return to femininity that was eagerly adopted by women who had had enough of the Make Do And Mend years – not to mention the drab garb of standard munitions-factory wear.

LEFT Memorable events such as wars, royal visits, new inventions and changing fashions have long provided fodder for wallpaper design, including striking aeronautical images.

'All [life] is pattern but we can't always see the pattern when we're part of it.'
BELVA PLAIN

During the 1950s cultural changes provided a wealth of ideas for wallpaper design. Thanks to a significant increase in disposable income, business in the travel and leisure industry began to boom, inspiring a raft of lifestyle images portraying groups of people promenading in the park, walking their dogs, or soaking up the sun outside French bistros. Motifs such as carafes, cocktail glasses and bottles of foreign wine also signalled a return to the good life. The 1950s was the first decade of television, with 'TVs' becoming a standard fixture in middle-class homes across the Western world. As a result, wallpapers at this time featured the jaunty Vs of television aerials.

The space race was the dominant theme for current-events wallpapers in the 1960s. Fired by the Russian launch of Sputnik 1 in 1957 – the first vehicle to travel beyond the earth's atmosphere – the

OPPOSITE Papers that were patterned with rockets were extremely popular during the 1960s, as the space race gathered momentum.

RIGHT As the most famous band in history, it's not surprising that portraits of the Fab Four appeared on wallpaper.

BELOW Hugely popular from the mid-1970s onwards, the craze for skateboarding took the Western world by storm.

fascination with lunar travel was further fuelled by the launch of astronaut Yuri Gagarin into space in 1962. In the same year, the young President, John F Kennedy prophesied that American astronauts would walk on the moon before the close of the decade; when Neil Armstrong fulfilled this prediction in 1969, a galaxy of moon-landing designs followed.

The 1960s was also notable for the explosion of youth culture, which manifested itself in funky clothing, accessible artwork and, thanks to the Beatles, music with mass appeal. Not surprisingly, the Fab Four were immortalized on wallpaper and the images act as nostalgic reminders of the century's most innovative and exciting decade.

NEW DIRECTIONS

The twentieth century saw many artists seeking to bridge the gap between the fine and decorative arts. In the early 1920s Belgian painter René Magritte produced abstract wallpaper patterns in bright colours, while artists such as Alexander Calder, Graham Sutherland and Andy Warhol also produced wallpapers for the sheer pleasure of pattern making.

Architects working in the the nineteenth and twentieth century were producing wallpapers, too. Influential figures such as A W N Pugin, Charles Rennie Mackintosh and Frank Lloyd Wright all created designs that complemented their architectural style, while Le Corbusier designed papers with the specific intention of manipulating interior space. In 1931 he teamed up with manufacturing company Salubra

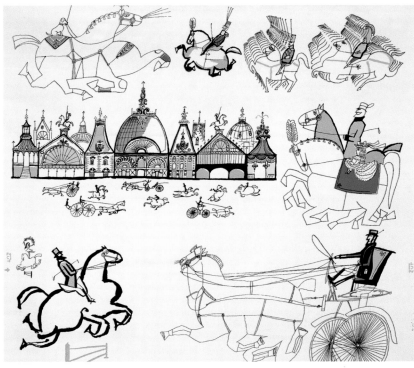

ABOVE Known for his cartoonlike wallpapers, American designer Saul Steinberg here playfully portrayed horses and carriages on Fifth Avenue in New York.

LEFT Better known for his surreal depictions of seagulls and men in bowler hats, Belgian painter René Magritte started his career designing wallpaper during the early 1920s.

to produce his collection of single-coloured papers. Created specifically for 'architectural animation', the designs were named Space, Sky, Velvet and Sand, in order to describe their mural effect. With his second wallpaper series, which he produced in 1959, Le Corbusier introduced bolder marble patterns in various colours. These papers could be hung in horizontal or vertical arrangements, and were intended to become the dramatic focus of an entire wall.

The concept of wallpaper as an art form also appeals to contemporary artists. In 1982, Bridget Riley hung screen-printed panels depicting her famous stripes on the walls of a corridor in the Royal Liverpool Hospital, brightening up the dreary décor with bands of colour in blue, ochre, pink and white. Controversial British artist, Damien Hirst, has also produced wallpaper designs including Lysergic Acid Diethylamide, which features multi-coloured spots, and Pharmaceuticals, a busy pill-popping pattern.

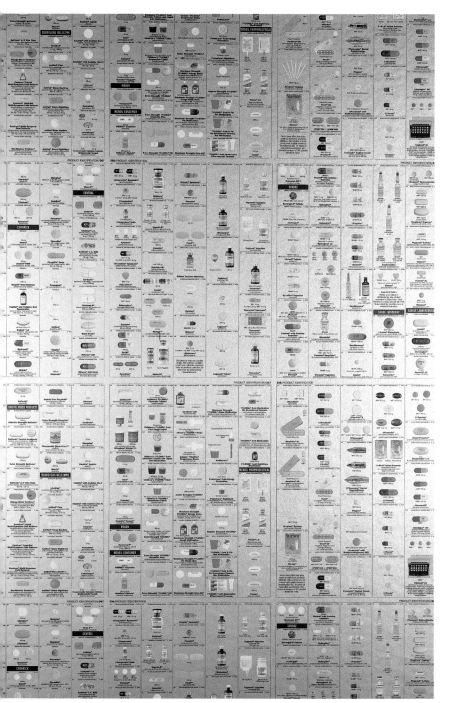

By contrast, fellow Brit artist, Sarah Lucas, created her Tits in Space paper using a looser image on a larger scale. Her work illustrates a new attitude to wallpaper design, recently made possible by techniques in computer-driven technology. By the same token, a fresh approach to block- and screen-printing allows designers to produce images that cover an entire wall with no visible repeat. As a result, some contemporary artists are turning their paintings into wallpaper, while a growing number of modern art galleries are choosing to show artists' wallpapers as exhibitable items in their own right.

LEFT Wallpapers by contemporary artists include Damien Hirst's pill-popping pattern, Pharmaceuticals.

ABOVE Tits in Space by British artist Sarah Lucas offers a raunchy alternative to traditional wallpaper motifs.

'IN GENERAL, MY PAINTINGS ARE MULTIFOCAL. YOU CAN'T CALL IT UNFOCUSED SPACE, BUT NOT BEING FIXED TO A SINGLE FOCUS IS VERY MUCH OF OUR TIME.'
BRIDGET RILEY

OPPOSITE Wallpaper that has been designed to imitate real materials such as stainless steel offers a realistic but much less expensive alternative to the genuine article.

LEFT Following advances in computer technology, modern wallpaper motifs are now available on a bigger, brighter and more exuberant scale than was previously thought possible.

NEW TECHNOLOGY

Until recently, wallpaper has been an attractive but restrictive medium, due to the constraints imposed by the repeat image. But now an increasing number of contemporary wallpaper designers are challenging conventional methods of production in order to create looser, more fluid styles that give greater artistic scope. The innovative creations that have emerged from this directive are partly the result of new pattern-making techniques, which have increased the opportunities for designers to produce papers that do not present an obviously repetitive image. To achieve this, two rolls of wallpaper are printed with slightly different designs and then hung in alternate strips. This uncomplicated method gives the impression of the pattern unfolding around the room in a seemingly random fashion. Not only that, but the advent of new techniques has also enabled the creation of innovative designs, which range from papers sporting textured hearts to swirly patterns that glow in the dark.

Computer technology has also revolutionized wallpaper design, allowing for the depiction of motifs and patterns on a much larger scale. At the touch of a button, a favoured image such as a vivid flower head can be dramatically enlarged in order to produce an abstract mass of colours and shapes. In addition, computer-aided technology enables the use of photographic images, which can be manipulated on screen in a similar fashion and then printed on to wallpaper. These kinds of papers lend themselves well to artistic application as a single strip depicting an outsize image is liable to create a greater impact than a room papered wall-to-wall with repetitive motifs.

Wallpaper

Fashion hip strips

OPPOSITE An accessories designer first and foremost, Neisha Crosland combines graphic cool with full-on femininity in her wallpaper designs.

RIGHT By transferring their fabric designs on to wallpaper, designers Eley Kishimoto guarantee that walls are as well-dressed as wardrobes.

FASHION GOES TO THE WALL

Thanks to an increasing number of fashion designers launching homeware collections, the trend for dressy interiors has gone from strength to strength. Not content with producing the occasional cable-knit cushion or selection of sleek ceramics, designers such as Dolce e Gabbana, Eley Kishimoto and Ralph Lauren have all produced wallpapers with a sassy sartorial twist. Better still, choosing a fashionable theme for your walls presents an exciting variety of choice:

take your pick from styles that range from classical to street, hippie to disco and glamorous to utilitarian. And if you're a label junky, it is even possible to clad your walls with trendy fashion logos.

In addition, there are numerous fabric-look fashion papers – from classic tartan to distressed denim and raunchy lace – with which to adorn your walls; whatever your dress sense, you can be sure there is a paper to cover it.

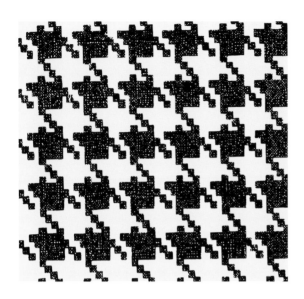

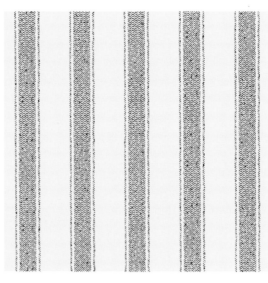

FAR LEFT Houndstooth patterns, either in graphic black and white or pastel shades such as primrose yellow or baby blue, are an effective way to give interiors an elegant update.

LEFT To create a seriously urbane look, choose striped papers in sober colours and combine with dark leather furnishings.

THE CLASSIC LOOK

OPPOSITE Creased-silk-effect wallpaper is a perfect ploy for creating textural contrast in interiors, while the raised folds introduce a feeling of depth.

Buy a well-cut pair of black trousers and you furnish your wardrobe with a classy staple that is guaranteed to survive the vagaries of fashion. This approach also works well when it comes to classic wallpaper designs, which will still look fresh and contemporary long after their initial pasting.

PASTEL STRIPES

Ralph Lauren's pastel stripes are an ideal way to dress up a room without the overall effect appearing too showy. As with his casual button-down Oxford shirts, the subtle appeal of Lauren's wallpapers, which come in similar stripes of baby blue, pale pink and peppermint on a white background, is an informal, chic one. Team with white or cream furnishings to create an airy spacious effect, or combine with faded florals to conjure a summer-house-in-the-Hamptons look.

PINSTRIPES

Pinstripes introduce a more formal tone, thanks to their association with businessmen in suits.

The monochrome variety, as seen in Casa Zegna (Ermenegildo Zegna's home furnishings range), is ideal for creating an urbane bachelor-pad look. Deploy it in the bathroom to provide a macho complement to chrome fixtures and fittings, or hang it in a sitting room and team with lounge-lizard-style furnishings such as a hi-tech music system, smoked-glass table and black leather sofa. To summon a feeling of grandeur, use a pinstripe paper in jewel-bright shades; thin white lines on a ruby-red background provide a wonderfully opulent look in a formal dining room, for example, especially if you combine the design with gilt mirrors or ponderous oil portraits. Alternatively, paper a man's dressing room in navy and white stripes to create a smart tailored look.

HOUNDSTOOTH

Vaunted by Coco Chanel – and reminiscent of fabulous 1940s fashion – wallpaper sporting a houndstooth pattern gives an elegant air of sartorial chic. If you want to make a really dramatic fashion statement, paper a small room with jagged checks in black and white – bathrooms are ideal, for the reflective surfaces of mirror and chrome serve as instruments to highlight the graphic effect. Another option is to use houndstooth in tasteful colourways such as pale lemon or classic camel to give drawing rooms or guest bedrooms a dignified period feel.

PLEATED SILK

Particularly popular in early nineteenth-century France, skillfully shaded silk trompe l'oeil wallpaper has been reinterpreted to suit the subtler demands of modern interiors. Replacing the painted swathes and swags of yore, the irregular creases of today's papers mimic the soft fall of designer silks such as Issey Miyake's Pleats Please collection. The illusion of depth and interest created by the two-dimensional folds provides an ideal backdrop in minimalist interiors where texture provides the main decorative theme, while a dressier look is achieved through the addition of key accessories such as a diamanté photograph frame or shawl sewn with delicate seed pearls.

LACE

Trompe l'oeil lace papers were also sought after in nineteenth-century France. Like imitation drape designs, these patterns were loud and intrusive – their intricate detailing and flouncy ribbons giving the sort of frothy look that contemporary interiors strive to avoid. By contrast, modern lace papers have undergone a minimalist makeover – with the new look more sexy suspenders than prim petticoats To get a seductive boudoir feel, simply paper one wall with an intricate black-lace design and leave the others plain; then dress the bed with sumptuous silk comforters, slippery satin sheets and the occasional chinoiserie cushion. Alternatively, go for vintage style and complement lace walls with dark furniture, velvet upholstery, paisley shawls and lots of bohemian fringing.

THE COUNTRY LOOK

TARTAN

Boldly checked patterns have long been a feature in interior design schemes, offering a dramatic design directive within a variety of different gridworks. A traditional fixture in Scottish baronial castles – tartan carpets and walls give instant Celtic confidence – plaid has lately been popularized by chic fashion houses such as Burberry and Daks, making it the epitome of cool. A fundamentally strong and dominant design, tartan is available in numerous colourways – from bold and dramatic to pale and interesting. Choose combinations such as soft fawn and heathery violet or moss green and mushroom for quiet areas such as bedrooms and studies; and stronger colour mixes like emerald green and midnight blue or scarlet and navy to create a sense of purpose and energy in transitional areas such as halls, landings and alongside stairways. Even in larger rooms such as sitting and dining areas, plaid is surprisingly easy to live with – once the initial sensation of being wrapped in a rug has worn off. For maximum effect, team tartan walls with soft furnishings in gently clashing checks.

TWEED

Wallpapers that depict woven fabrics such as tweed and herringbone are another option for those wishing to create interiors with a strong, sartorial feel. Far from being frumpy, these 'old-fashioned' papers have a fashionable 1940s appeal, while their neutral appearance is quietly conducive. Available in calming shades of buff, beige and biscuit, tweedy patterns give an effortlessly pulled-together effect, and look best in elegant drawing rooms with classically proportioned furniture and a muted palette of pastel hues. Another device is to use darker-coloured tweeds – bitter-chocolate brown and racing green are good choices – in halls and cloakrooms to create a hearty outdoors note combined with a playful fashion flick.

GINGHAM

Brightly checked gingham is another fashion fabric that translates effectively on to walls. Popular in the 1950s, thanks to Brigitte Bardot and her arsenal of checked bikinis, this simple design has a nostalgic down-home atmosphere and helps to imbue interiors with feelings of freshness and vitality. It is also possible to create a variety of different looks using gingham: mix it with vintage-style florals to bring a quaint country-cottage look or accentuate an existing colour scheme with checks in similar shades. For a simple Scandinavian air, combine gingham walls in red, green or mauve with minimalist furnishings – and leave it at that.

OPPOSITE TOP Tartan checks in a combination of earthy shades will help to imbue your living space with feelings of peace and tranquillity. Team with retro accessories for a reassuring vintage feeling or combine with ultra-modern furnishings to create a pleasing juxtaposition between charming tradition and twenty-first-century chic.

OPPOSITE BOTTOM For a spontaneous colour scheme, simply pick one or two shades from your wallcovering and use to link furnishings and accessories.

THE DISCO LOOK

GLITTER, SEQUINS AND NIGHTCLUB BLACK

Taking its cue from the fashion for all things sparkly, glitter wallpaper adds a disco dimension to modern interiors. Whether in delicate pastels or darker and more dramatic shades, twinkly walls are an effective way to light up your home – without the overall effect appearing too garish. That said, glitter papers do work best in small rooms. Although the glint is a subtle, almost subdued one, the novelty of these festive wallcoverings is best appreciated at close quarters. Choose sea-green sparkles for titchy bathrooms, primrose yellow for dingy hallways and milky white for a celestial effect in airy bedrooms. If your aim is to re-create the '60s glamour of Studio 54 in New York, cover your walls with liberally sprinkled black papers – and get on down …

Paper sporting sequins is another option for fashionistas who want to customize their walls as well as their wardrobes. But be warned, bespoke designs such as these don't come cheap. 'It's possible to sew any number of fashiony items on to wallpaper,' says British designer Tracy Kendall, who screen-prints her papers with delicate outlines before sewing on every button and bauble by hand. Three days of painstaking stitching produces about 3 m (10 ft) of paper, and clients are encouraged to contribute their own ideas – from neon flocking strewn with seed pearls to hippie lovebeads arranged within delicate paisley curls.

'One of the goals of life is to try and be in touch with one's most personal themes — the values, ideas, styles, colours that are the touchstones of one's own individual life, its real texture and substance.'

GLORIA VANDERBILT

LEFT Inexpensive and hard-wearing, Anaglypta papers are enjoying a resurgence in popularity. Available in white and cream, Anaglypta that is painted black gives a seductive clubby mood.

ABOVE Button-back satin designs offer a fast and effective solution for rooms in need of a glamorous update. Apply with caution, however, as a little goes a long way.

THE UTILITARIAN LOOK

CAMOUFLAGE

Combats, dog tags, S-belts – the fashion for Army-inspired clothes and accessories is an endlessly popular one. Little wonder, then, that camouflage wallpaper is winning the battle as the fashionista's favourite cover-up. But be prepared: this look is not for the faint-hearted; camouflage may blend in when you're crawling through the Amazon jungle, but stick it on your sitting-room walls and it screams for attention. With this proviso in mind, ensure success by reinforcing your combat walls with furnishings that have a complementary military link – a khaki-coloured carpet, a couple of canvas chairs and the odd bit of webbing should do the trick.

DENIM

A perennial leader in the fashion stakes, blue denim is also becoming a hot favourite in the home thanks to its casual loungy appearance. Better still, the current range of denim wallpapers runs the gamut from dark indigo to fashionably faded – with distressed, ripped and stonewashed styles also available. One of the main advantages of opting for denim walls is the ever-increasing number of jeans-style furnishings on the market. For a full-on look, go for cushions, curtains, beanbags, sheets, duvet covers, pillowcases and eiderdowns – all in dyed blue cotton. It is also easy to dress denim up or down thanks to its no-nonsense neutral appearance. In the same way that you might combine faded jeans with a pair of superglam slingbacks, you can twin distressed denim walls with a crystal chandelier, or pair smart indigo-style papers with slightly scuffed leather furniture. Alternatively, mix and match jeans walls with mohair, lace and neon brights to create a variety of different looks – from vintage to street.

ABOVE Perfect for combative types, camouflage wallpaper is not for the lily-livered. To complete the look, team with Astroturf flooring and canvas upholstery, preferably in khaki hues.

OPPOSITE Complement denim wallpaper with a selection of jeans-style furnishings, which include bedlinen, beanbags, cushions and curtains – and come in varying shades of blue.

'Mere colour, unspoiled by meaning, and unallied with definite form, can speak to the soul in a thousand different ways.' OSCAR WILDE

THE NEON LOOK

The craze for clothing that has been accessorized with brightly coloured details takes its cue from urban sportswear brands such as Nike, whose trainers, complete with fluorescent ticks, kickstarted a global trend. Nylon trackpants with neon stripes followed, along with acid-hued accessories including belts, badges and hairclips. But neon-coloured wallpaper? Surely this is taking the fluorescent thing a step too far? In fact, neon designs are among the best ways to give interiors a sense of space and depth. Available in purple, pink, orange and lime – and created to fade from saturated shades to delicate pastel hues – neon wallpaper is a brilliant way to open out dark dingy areas: deploy it in hallways where the fade-out effect can be fully appreciated, or hang it in domestic areas like kitchens – and enjoy the juxtaposition of everyday utensils with a spattering of fashion funk.

LEFT Inspired by the fashion for fluorescent detailing – particularly on trendy sportswear – neon-bright wallpaper is, literally, a brilliant way to open out dingy spaces. Designed to fade from saturated colour to gentle pastel hues, these papers also give a sense of space and depth.

THE FASHION-LABEL LOOK

Label junkies will love the Hysteric Glamour room at Hotel Pelirocco in Brighton on the south-east coast of Britain. Happily, this is a look that is easily imitated. To create your own fashion mecca, simply take a copy of your favourite logo – Fiorucci, Polo Ralph Lauren and Tommy Hilfiger are strong motifs – to a printing shop, get it enlarged and then paste it on to the walls. For a comprehensive look, it is also possible to have your chosen logo printed on plain cotton from which you can make up matching duvet covers, pillows, cushions, curtains and blinds.

BELOW The Hysteric Glamour room at Hotel Pelirocco in Brighton is an excellent example of how a fashion label can create a total design scheme. In this instance, the logo is featured on the sheets and blinds as well as on the walls.

RIGHT AND FAR RIGHT The realistic appearance and practicality of Deborah Bowness's quirky Hooks and Frocks wallpaper is strengthened by the addition of useable hooks for hanging up real, rather than photographed, items of clothing.

THE DRESSING-ROOM LOOK

For the fully-fledged fashionista, Deborah Bowness's Hooks and Frocks wallpaper is, quite simply, to die for. Developed by the British designer while she was still at art college, the idea of photographing domestic interiors – warts and all – came from six years of constantly moving to different rented accommodation. 'I wanted to personalize a space that wasn't really mine,' says Bowness, who subsequently photographed her clothes and bags, had the pictures enlarged and then pasted them on to strips of paper. The result is a fashionable three-dimensional collage in the style of a David Hockney montage – and the paper's usable hooks give an ingenious functional edge.

THE ACCESSORIZED LOOK

Whether you're putting the finishing touches to an outfit, or decorating the walls of your home, the power of a few good accessories should never be underestimated. If you're the type who prefers to concentrate attention on the trimmings rather than the main event, wallpapers with motifs such as sunglasses, jewellery or buttons are the ones to go for. Better still, it's possible to use these papers sparingly while still maintaining a fashionable front. Paper an alcove with Paloma Picasso's interlinking bracelet designs to achieve a subtle glinty look, or line the inside of a glass-fronted case with bejewelled bag motifs for a full-on fashion moment.

LEFT A selection of glitzy buttons that appear to have been randomly scattered across a neutral background makes an ideal 'accessories' paper for decorating small spaces – cosy niches, alcoves and walk-in wardrobes are ideal.

ABOVE Available in primary colours or graphic black and white, this sunglasses paper is both aesthetic and zany.

OPPOSITE Splendidly jewelled handbags, with intricate detailing to match, make a striking style statement.

Nature eco chic

THE INFLUENCE OF NATURE

Since the inception of wallpaper, the natural world has proved a rich source of inspiration for designers. In the seventeenth century Chinese patterns depicted birds, weeping willows and bamboo; these were followed in the eighteenth century by flowery papers in the style of Indian fabric, chintz or toile de Jouy. At the end of the nineteenth century, noted British and American designers such as A W N Pugin and Candace Wheeler favoured the Tudor rose and the honeybee, respectively.

Today the natural world wields as strong an influence on wallpaper design as it did in the past, although the emphasis now is as political as it is aesthetic. As the harmful side effects of consumerism and mass production put the world's natural resources increasingly under threat, environmental awareness has become a key issue for all of us. Not surprisingly, we want to celebrate the bounty of Mother Earth – and one way to do this is by furnishing our homes with eco-friendly materials. As a result, bamboo, felt and cork are all regaining credibility in contemporary interiors, while wallpaper designed on organic themes include contemporary chintz, weather-map designs and translucent papers threaded with seaweed.

CHINTZ

Taking its name from the Hindu word 'chint', meaning variegated, chintz first appeared in the West as cotton cloth imported from India. This glazed material was fast-printed with designs of flowers, birds and foliage and brought the abundance of nature into the home.

Chintz was introduced to Europe during the seventeenth century following the expansion of the Indo-European textile trade. Westerners loved the riotous patterns and generous employment of colour – and used the fabric for beds, windows and chair coverings as well as hanging it on their walls.

By 1775 copperplate and roller-printing machines that could produce chintz patterns cheaply were in common use in Europe, thus putting an end to India's trade monopoly. As the textiles industries started to flourish, chintz began to be exported in large quantities to America, the colonists having a preference for English fashions. There are records of London drapers in 1800 recommending to Americans 'packages' of coordinated chintzes, while French and English wallpaper manufacturers also picked up on the vogue for flamboyant designs and produced their own versions of chintz – sheets of patterned paper in soft earthy shades, often with a pale brown or tea-stained background, which was in sharp contrast to the brighter palette favoured by the American market.

OPPOSITE The block-printed motifs of this modern wallpaper have a stylized, faintly Art Nouveau, feel.

BELOW Combining a larger floral print with a smaller one is a tried-and-tested design ploy, helping to divide different areas within a room.

HOW TO MIX AND MATCH FLORALS

- Mixing patterns is an excellent way to provide depth and interest in a room, even if your interior is on the mean side. To prevent confusion, choose a selection of designs that are similar in terms of colour, mood or type – but steer clear of likeness in scale.

- To get an idea of how different patterns will work together, assemble samples of wallpaper or swatches of fabric and try out your proposed combination on a small scale before you embark on the real thing.

- There should be some link between designs in terms of colour and tone. One pattern may be multicoloured, another feature a dominant colour from the first together with white, and a third display a duet of two toning shades.

- Look at your pattern combination from the point of view of scale. Two big patterns will work together only if they are similar in content; otherwise, the effect will tire the eyes. Conversely, geometric and floral patterns work well together provided there is a difference in scale – a smaller check with a larger floral design, for example.

CONTEMPORARY FLORALS

SHABBY CHIC

A key element of the look known as shabby chic is purposely faded florals, which are guaranteed to survive the vagaries of fashion. Taking its inspiration from the Victorian interpretation of early Eastern chintz designs, where blowsy cabbage roses, giant lilies and sinuous ribbons replaced the original birds, flowers and fruit, the timeless charm of vintage-style florals provides the perfect backdrop for bedrooms and living areas, where it creates an air of faded grandeur. Moreover, thanks to their subtle washed-out appearance, the large rambling designs of contemporary chintz wallpapers create a relaxed lived-in feel rather than a frantic claustrophobic one.

NEW ROMANTIC

Springing from the itsy-bitsy florals that were popular in 1940s interiors, today's spriggy papers are reminiscent of the Make Do and Mend years. Retaining their original rustic charm, the modern take on sweet floral knots forgoes the pastel pinks and primrose yellows of yesteryear in favour of a bolder palette of purple, red and fuchsia pink. Spriggy papers work best in small areas where their fresh appeal can be properly appreciated – and they can also be used to decorate niches, alcoves and window recesses. Alternatively, line a cleaning cupboard with titchy florals and enjoy the juxtaposition of domestic tools with delicate bouquets.

MODERN RUSTIC

This look twins nostalgic rose motifs with graphic shapes and a bright saturated palette. Reminiscent of 1950s design, which combined postwar optimism with the influence of abstract artists such as Joan Miró and Alexander Calder, polka dots – from teensy spots to solid spheres – are a particularly popular motif, along with calyx patterns and large

grids. Modern rustic-style wallpapers are best used in small rooms – cloakrooms, walk-in wardrobes and laundry rooms are all ideal – as their bold design and bright palette will appear overly frenetic in larger living areas, which are likely to be filled with more furniture and furnishings.

FAR LEFT It is possible to mix flower patterns as long as designs are similar in colour, type and scale.

LEFT The pink bricks of the fireplace surround

prevent the overblown wallpaper pattern from appearing old-fashioned.

BELOW Bold floral motifs in delicate colours give an elegant, romantic feel.

REALISM

Thanks to digital imaging (see page 29), floral wallcoverings are enjoying a fabulously modern makeover. In a radical departure from the rambling patterns and repetitive motifs witnessed in the past, the new-look florals feature single photographic images enlarged by up to a hundred times. The effect is strikingly realistic, making these papers ideal for modern interiors where the décor is minimal and the furniture simply designed.

OPPOSITE The realistic appearance of this dramatic floral pattern takes the eye beyond the flat surface of the wall, while the hydrangea-blue palette is compounded by the similarly coloured bed covering.

ABOVE LEFT AND RIGHT This modern version of single rose heads is reminiscent of the Art Deco period when floral designs were rigorously stylized and roses were a much-favoured motif.

HANGING BOLD FLORALS

- Bold florals are a great way to correct a room's architectural defects, as the directional stress of the pattern takes the eye beyond the flat surface of the wall, creating interest and depth.
- If you want to keep walls unobtrusive, search for a pattern that works all over and does not have pronounced lines.
- To create an aesthetic architectural effect, choose a paper with an easy balance of horizontal, vertical and oblique lines.
- For a peaceful look, go for a design with calming horizontal lines.
- To counter rigidity, select a soft fluid pattern.
- Use branching diagonal patterns in stairways and halls to lead the eye naturally upwards.
- A large pattern need not necessarily overpower the proportions of a room. Choose a pale colourway in order to reduce the impact of a dominant design.

'There are always flowers for those who want to see them.'
HENRI MATISSE

RIGHT Far from appearing old-fashioned, the Gothic appeal of this modern thistle design is entirely up-to-the-minute, thanks to the bold palette, which mixes red and purple to dramatic effect.

VEGETATIVE

The father of organic wallpaper design, William Morris's love affair with the natural world inspired 41 wallpapers and five ceiling papers – all depicting stylized flowers, trees, fruit and birds in varying permutations and colourways.

Morris designed his first wallpapers – Daisy, Trellis and Pomegranate – between 1864 and 1866. Preferring to hand-block his patterns rather than adopt the faked realism of machine-produced papers popular at the time, his continuous flowing lines give a sense of movement and luminosity that revolutionized the art of pattern-making and altered the course of Western design in the process.

Morris's later designs – including Jasmine, Willow Bough, Vine, Scroll, Acanthus and Larkspur – all have a similarly vibrant appeal. In addition to helping immortalize the wildflowers of England's water meadows and country gardens, their look of spontaneous growth retains its popularity to this day, imbuing modern interiors with a sense of energy and immediacy. And while the boldly graphic designs of papers such as Pomegranate have a contemporary feel that would not look out of place in a modern city apartment, patterns such as the frondy leaves of Willow Bough (opposite) are instantly updated by the use of funky colours. The British manufacturer Sanderson still produces Morris designs using the original blocks – with colours including three shades of green, as well as wine, terracotta, brown and blue. Morris designs can also be customized in a colour of your choice, although this is extremely expensive.

LEFT Foliage that has been abstracted to resemble a collection of scribbly loops still has a basically vegetative look.

OPPOSITE William Morris's Willow Bough print, complemented by a few simple furnishings, looks fresh and contemporary.

OPPOSITE Oversized feather motifs work especially well in minimalist settings.

a spontaneous feel of naturalism into interiors.

RIGHT The fine detail of this shell-patterned paper is perfect for adding interest to stark modern spaces.

BELOW Decorative pebbles and stones are a great way to introduce

FOUND OBJECTS

PEBBLES

In tune with the lasting fashion for Zen-style living, wallpaper featuring found objects such as stones and pebbles is guaranteed to imbue your space with a sense of organic naturalism. Not only are the irregular shapes of pebbles a great way to give a spontaneous feel, but the immutable presence of stone in your interiors will also help to make your space feel more grounded and peaceful.

SHELLS

Unbelievably beautiful as well as endlessly varied, the popularity of wallpapers depicting delicate shell motifs continues to endure. Their aesthetic appeal aside, shell designs also help to evoke happy memories such as holidays spent in far-flung locations or childhood visits to the sea. As a result, these wallpapers tend to work best in bathrooms and restrooms, where their associations with water can be fully appreciated.

FEATHERS

The main advantage of wallpapers featuring feather images is their ability to imbue interiors with a sense of lightness and optimism. A favourite motif with contemporary designers, wallpapers sporting feather patterns are available in a variety of cool modern colours including yellow, pink, purple and blue. These papers achieve their full potential when hung in large airy rooms where their ephemeral beauty and delicate detailing can be displayed to best advantage.

'I believe in God, only I spell it Nature.'
'Study nature, love nature, stay close to nature. It will never fail you.'
FRANK LLOYD WRIGHT

ORGANIC

One of the most effective ways to create an organic feel in the home is through the use of natural wallcoverings. The irregular weave of raffia, grasscloth and hessian papers has a wonderfully textural appeal, helping to confer a sensuous minimalism that is perfectly in tune with the back-to-basics look of contemporary interiors.

RAFFIA

Made from dried and woven palm leaves, raffia wallpaper is an excellent means of bringing the outside in, creating a rough basketweave appearance that is undeniably tactile. Better still, raffia papers have jettisoned their 'pale and interesting' image for a brighter look that includes designs in pink, mulberry and tangerine.

HESSIAN

Reminiscent of hippie 1960s style, hessian wallpaper is also enjoying a revival thanks to its ability to imbue interiors with feelings of warmth and harmony. Available in neutral shades of buff, beige and biscuit, hessian papers have a robust texture that provides the perfect complement to smooth metal or glass furnishings.

GRASSCLOTH

Grasscloths have been used as wallcoverings for centuries, particularly in Japan and Korea. As a result, many of the grasscloth papers included in Western interiors are imported from the Far East, although some are produced in Europe. Ranging from slightly textured to truly bumpy,

grass papers give rooms a marvellously organic feel. The fibrous texture is enhanced by the varying thicknesses of each grass blade, while pieces of bark and leaves which have been interwoven give an invitingly rough-and-ready quality. In order to create a natural haven for the senses, combine grasscloth papers with simple wood furnishings and organic fabrics, including raw silk, linen or unbleached cotton.

SEAWEED

Minimalists will love the almost translucent appearance of undyed Japanese paper, which is threaded with delicate strands of seaweed. For best results, use these designs in rooms that have been pared down, in order that their ephemeral intricacy can be properly appreciated.

BAMBOO

Papers imitating bamboo – one of the fastest-growing and most sustainable plants on the planet – have a remarkable three-dimensional appearance and a warm naturalistic quality. Use them to give rooms an exotic Far Eastern flavour or a feeling of serene tranquillity.

OPPOSITE The beautifully streamlined effect of this space is due to grasscloth wallpaper being pasted over the door as well as the walls. The natural theme is further consolidated through the addition of a silken fur rug that, in turn, provides a pleasing textural counterpoint to the rougher surface of the wallcovering.

BELOW Contemporary interpretations of toile de Jouy are plainer and more abstract than the traditional variety.

TOILE DE JOUY

Originally serving as an expensive fabric used to decorate the walls or, alternatively, cover sofas, chairs and beds, toile de Jouy's pictorial patterns were inspired by the exotic designs that appeared on cotton cloths imported from India during the seventeenth century. In 1760 a factory manufacturing similar types of fabric was founded at Jouy-en-Josas, a little village to the south-west of Paris. During the eighteenth century wallpapers that replicated the mainly pastoral themes typical of toile de Jouy began to be produced.

Part of the appeal of toile de Jouy lies in its versatility. Capable of giving a crisp cottagey feel or a grandly opulent one, these papers can be used in cosy bedrooms or elegant drawing rooms alike. Better still, because of its single-colour scheme, it

is also possible to coordinate toile de Jouy wallpaper with similarly patterned fabrics without the end result appearing too over the top.

Originally available in dusty rose, faded blue and sepia on a natural background, contemporary versions include sharper shades such as emerald green, chocolate brown and tangerine orange. In addition, backgrounds are occasionally colourwashed to give further interest.

OPPOSITE Grey toile suits minimalist interiors perfectly, providing the ideal complement to sleek accessories and cool contemporary furniture.

ABOVE Jungle patterns are a popular theme for toile designs, while a palette of stronger colours replaces the dusty hues of yesteryear.

JUNGLE

During the second half of the nineteenth century, the development of roller-printing techniques and the introduction of synthetic dyes made it much easier for wallpaper manufacturers on both sides of the Atlantic to produce sophisticated but reasonably inexpensive pictorial patterns. Favoured subject matter included rural landscapes, scenes from industry and commerce, significant military and political events and motifs derived from chinoiserie and japanoiserie. In addition, images of wild animals from the jungles and plains of central and southern Africa were also popular and included exuberant representations of elephants, tigers, lions, parrots and monkeys.

Depictions of jungle animals also appeared on toile de Jouy designs, which were produced at the famous French factory in Jouy-en-Josas. Apart from chinoiserie, the most widely favoured subject matter for designs were romanticized or idealized scenes of rural life, and images of magical faraway lands. Not surprisingly, the vivid enchantment of jungle life with all its many connotations of colour, danger and exoticism was an endlessly appealing theme.

The call of the wild is still making itself heard to this day; contemporary designs feature a variety of jungle animals (monkeys are a particular favourite) peering out from the leafy boughs of tropical trees.

ABOVE Jungle scenes are a popular theme on toile de Jouy papers, which traditionally presented a romanticized vision of foreign lands.

LEFT Modern depictions of jungle life contain an abundance of lush leafy foliage.

OPPOSITE Wallpapers featuring the elegant fronds of palm leaves are currently enjoying a resurgence in popularity.

THE ELEMENTS

SKY

The custom of decorating ceilings and walls with wispy floating clouds is not a new one. Adopted by the great Italian masters of trompe l'oeil painting such as Tiepolo, sky papers are an effective way of bringing the outside in, as well as helping to create a relaxing environment. As a result, there are now numerous variations available: for a truly realistic look, choose digitally produced designs that give a photographic effect on a large scale, or opt for papers that have been hand-blocked so that each cloud is an original – rather than a repeated – motif. Sunny sky papers are a great way to make interiors seem brighter, lighter and more airy. Particularly effective in bathrooms, where the bather can wallow for hours while gazing into the blue yonder, they also enhance bedrooms and studies, imparting a calming meditative mood.

NIGHT SKY

Night-sky wallpapers give an entirely different effect from sunny-day designs, enveloping interiors with a sense of magic and mystery as opposed to creating feelings of lightness and space. Available in a variety of guises – from moody indigo dotted with pinpricks of silver light to inky swatches decorated with vivid planets – night-sky papers work to stunning effect in dining rooms, where their celestial influence is greatly enhanced by the addition of candlelight. Alternatively, use them on bedroom ceilings to create a romantic and dreamy atmosphere.

OPPOSITE Night-sky paper, studded with pinpricks of coloured light, provides the perfect coverage for bedroom ceilings.

THIS PAGE Wallpaper depicting blue sky and scudding clouds is one of the most effective ways of bringing the outside in.

WEATHER

The latest twist on traditional cloud wallpapers are weather-map designs, which give a bolder, more graphic effect. Meteorological patterns such as groups of small curving arrows depicting wind-force strength are great for adding a sense of energy and movement to walls, while gently curvilinear isobar designs give a calmer, more cosmic effect.

MAPS

Perfect for globetrotters and armchair travellers alike, map designs are guaranteed to give your interiors a sense of freedom and adventure. Available in ancient dusty colours or brighter, more immediate ones, map designs can either be used to blend in with existing furnishings or to act as a room's main focus. Use them in transitional areas such as hallways or stairways, to introduce a lively itinerant feeling.

LEFT The graphic appearance of weather charts provide a variety of motifs for wallpaper designs. Use arrows illustrating wind force to generate a sense of movement, and isobar patterns to create a more peaceful feel.

OPPOSITE Covering walls with large-scale map designs is an inexpensive way to decorate your home. Use sepia styles to re-create the glamour of travel in bygone days, or brighter ones to inspire a sense of freedom and adventure.

'There are painters who transform the sun into a yellow spot, but there are others who ... transform a yellow spot into the sun.'

PABLO PICASSO

Realism faking it

IMITATION SKINS

Wallpaper that simulates hard-wearing natural surfaces such as wood, stone, brick and bamboo is not a new concept. For hundreds of years, homeowners have used fake papers as a less expensive option to the real thing, and the trend continues to this day. From faux-leopard-print designs to pretend pebbledash, faking it is a fast and effective way to inject an unusual measure of interest into your interiors. Better still, the new raft of imitation papers are so cleverly designed that it's hard to tell the real thing from the fake one.

HIDE AND SEEK

Animal prints have long been fashionable in home furnishings. At the turn of the twentieth century, when big-game hunting was at its height, tiger- and leopard-skin rugs were prized flooring features in the drawing rooms of the international elite. Similarly, wastepaper bins balanced on elephant feet were sought after by affluent homeowners wanting to celebrate the remaining years of colonial rule.

Today stag's heads are a ubiquitous feature in the cavernous hallways of country houses across Europe and America. However, the rest of the (mainly) animal-loving public prefer to furnish their homes with imitation skins – a trend originally inspired by the ponyskin clogs and mock-croc belts witnessed on the catwalk. Sexy and sybaritic, the fashion for hide on the home front clawed its way into our consciousness with a few, very select, accessories. As fur-trimmed cushions, leather drawer pulls and leopard-print lampshades were hunted down by homeowners keen to cash in on the latest look, canny designers focused their attention on what was clearly a burgeoning trend, producing more

OPPOSITE To create a wild interior, use wallpaper imitating animal skins – choose anything from zebra or leopard to alligator, crocodile or snake. For full-on flamboyance, hang it from floor to ceiling and team with opulent funiture and furnishings.

substantial pieces such as leather beanbags, suede floor cubes, bear-skin bed throws and chairs covered in cowhide.

ANIMAL-PRINT PAPERS

While furniture, flooring, bedding and accessories were all being made fit for the jungle, walls remained unaccountably blank – until now, that is. The last word in hip homeware, the new raft of wacky wallcoverings includes a veritable menagerie of animal hide – with leopard-, zebra-, snake- and crocodile-skin prints all ripe and ready for a pasting. The palette for animal skins has also been updated. The contemporary palette includes jungle green, brilliant turquoise and modern metallics tinted with a funky iridescent sheen, reminiscent of an oil slick.

DOS AND DON'TS WITH HIDE

• A busy animal print will work better in a small room such as a study or walk-in closet than in a larger one, where even a strong pattern can be lost.

• Beware of using a busy two-tone print in restful areas, as it can have an overly stimulating effect. Instead, use hide in activity zones such as kitchens, laundry rooms or dining areas.

• Be bold: a full-on approach usually works better than a half-hearted one when it comes to animal hide, so take a deep breath and go for comprehensive coverage.

LEFT AND RIGHT
Stone fragments in
a pattern of ever-
increasing circles are
reminiscent of the
ordered simplicity of
a formal Zen garden,
and give similar feelings
of calm and tranquillity
as well as introducing
a textural element.

MASONRY

SURREAL STONE

The best thing about fake-stone wallpapers is the
sheer variety of finishes available. From veiny marble
to plain masonry blocks, and speckled granite to cool
concrete, there's a look to suit every interior. Not
only that, but fake-stone papers are extremely
convincing – their realistic appearance having been
honed over hundreds of years of imitative practice.

The natural colouring of stone wallpaper is
in perfect accord with the minimalist appeal of
contemporary interiors. Far from complicating your
space with an extra decorative layer, plain stone
papers actually emphasize the stripped-back look.
For example, papers that have been fabricated to
resemble concrete give a refined sense of industrial
chic and work brilliantly in urban homes with an
abundance of light and space. Similarly, clean-cut

blocks in large open-plan areas help to evoke a cool
spartan feel, while fake-stone wall designs – achieved
through the addition of a pale grid representing
mortar – give a sense of space and symmetry, and
are particularly effective in formal areas such as
hallways and vestibules.

Stone-effect papers also provide an excellent
opportunity to create a decorative contrast: modern
prints hanging on a seemingly ancient masonry wall
supplies an aesthetic balance of old and new, for
example, while the juxtaposition of roughly hewn
blocks with smooth curvilinear furniture gives an
equally pleasing effect. Another idea is to pair like
with like – stone-effect walls with flagged-stone
floors brings a wonderfully grounded feeling, and
the look is softened through the addition of fleecy
cushions, a goatskin rug or mohair throw.

'Space and light and order. Those are the things that men need just as much as they need bread or a place to sleep.' LE CORBUSIER

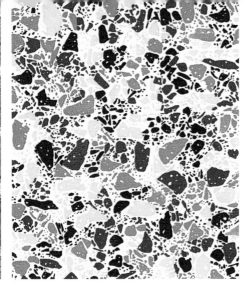

GRAVEL

Suggestive of Japanese pebble gardens, gravel wallpaper is a novel way of bringing the outside in. Rough and textural, these designs have a modern, edgy look and add a wonderfully tactile element to interiors. Not only that, but the inherently subtle quality of today's gravel papers allows them to be used in any room without appearing overly dominant. Pair their rough modernity with elegant antique furniture in a drawing room, for contrast, or combine with Astroturf flooring to give a full-on organic feel.

Gravel wallpapers also provide a complementary backdrop for funky furnishings. To create a smart, macho look, choose a dark shade and combine it with concrete flooring – topped with a sheepskin rug to soften the look – grey suede sofas and lots of smoked glass. Paler shades work best when they are offset by the clean lines of mid-century modern furnishings – a Panton table or Eames chair will provide the perfect foil, for example.

Gravel papers in zany colourways such as purple or orange offer the perfect excuse for a smattering of kitsch furnishings: hippie-trippy lava lamps, saggy baggy beanbags or a trailing flex dotted with multicoloured fairy lights are all ideal. Alternatively, use bright gravel designs to create a focal point – and keep additional furniture and furnishings to a minimum.

FAUX BRICKS

The popularity of fake-brick papers springs from the fashion for traditional loft living, where the structural elements of a building – including iron roof girders and brick walls – are often left exposed. This raw state of affairs is immensely appealing to those with deconstructive leanings, but, sadly, inhabiting thousands of feet of empty warehouse space is not an option for the majority of homeowners.

It is possible to achieve an edgy urban look by papering your walls with faux-brick styles, however. Just remember that these truly realistic papers are best used with a good deal of restraint – the end result could seem overpowering if they are used on every wall in a room. Instead, in the kitchen, for example, just paper the wall behind the cooker with a bold brick print and leave the others plain. This will give a fabulous workaday feel, as well as providing a textural interplay between rough and smooth. Another idea is to paper angled or sloping walls with fake-brick designs to emphasize their lack of uniformity and create a quirky feature.

The slightly kitsch appearance of fake brick papers can also be exploited: to add a surprise element, paste a striking red-brick style on to a door, or hang a single strip down the middle of a plain wall to create a graphic focal point. Alternatively, paste a fake-brick border around a modern fireplace to make a gently ironic frame.

ABOVE Contemporary wallpapers imitating various types of stone including granite, brick, marble and terrazzo are amazingly realistic, and offer a less expensive alternative to home-owners who want to give their interiors a sense of gravitas, but are unable to afford the real thing.

OPPOSITE Gravel papers have a modern edgy appearance, giving walls a fabulously rugged appeal as well as providing the perfect backdrop for a variety of hip furnishings.

was the most sought after. These days wood-effect papers are much less complicated. In tune with the fashion for living in a stripped-back environment, many simply resemble plain planks – albeit with an interesting textural grain and realistic-looking raised finish. Thus, contemporary wallpaper manufacturers tend to keep their faux papers simple, as an endlessly repeating pattern of identical grain markings instantly negates the sense of organic naturalism.

Happily, the prodigious variety of fake-wood designs available enables the creation of umpteen different looks: use faux-tongue-and-groove boards to give a linear look that is calm and cohesive, pale papers such as imitation maple or ash to open out small dingy interiors, and darker gnarled ones to make larger areas feel cosier and more intimate. Further options include hanging whitewashed-wood papers to create an airy romantic ambience, beech strips to give a clean contemporary effect, honey-toned woods to conjure an atmosphere that is warm and inviting, and rougher driftwood styles for a natural back-to-basics look.

IMITATION BAMBOO

Appearing regularly on wallpaper since the sixteenth century when beautifully painted panels depicting Chinese life were first imported to Europe from the Far East, bamboo designs have undergone numerous style changes over the years, from realistic depictions of the graceful swaying form to stylized leaves in glinty metallics. Contemporary designers have taken this much-loved motif a step further, producing realistic imitations of split bamboo with a wonderfully three-dimensional effect. The clean linearity of bamboo stems – set either vertically or horizontally – has a delightfully calming effect, imbuing rooms with a sense of order and serenity. Fake-bamboo designs also provide a fabulously textural look that is optimized when teamed with organic accessories such as a vase of flowers.

ILLUSORY WOOD

For hundreds of years, wood-effect wallpaper has proved itself as a stalwart decorating device. In the eighteenth and nineteenth centuries, designs combed by hand or block-printed imitated wainscoting or carved wood panelling, while new papers were constantly being produced in order to keep up with the vagaries of fashionable wood choices: oak, teak and mahogany all enjoyed periods as the grain du jour, helping to imbue interiors with a sense of timeless grandeur in the days when an ornate look

OPPOSITE AND LEFT Contemporary papers imitating the grain, knots and whorls of real wood give a naturalistic feel and complement today's fuss-free interiors.

BELOW Wood-effect wallpaper does not have to look rustic. Team it with retro furnishings and natural materials such as felt and stone for a funky eclectic look.

LEFT Modern trompe l'oeil is light and sketchy, and gives walls a subtle sense of interest.

RIGHT Offering an instantly cerebral mood, wallpaper patterned with literary tomes re-creates the peaceful ambience of public reading rooms.

FAR RIGHT Wallpaper imitating the appearance of crushed paper provides an ironic reinterpretation of traditional designs.

REPRO BOOKS

Thanks to their attractive appearance, books have constituted a much-loved decorating device for centuries. Not only does a mix of hard and soft backs arranged along the length of a wall engender reassuring feelings of warmth and homeliness, but the presence of books can also be used as a clever design ploy, helping to scale down large or high-ceilinged rooms or lend weight to smaller or less remarkable ones. That said, many of us do not have enough books to make a worthwhile feature of them. Alternatively, we may not have enough space to accommodate a bulky bookcase but would still like to furnish our rooms with the cerebral serenity of numerous literary texts.

In these instances, wallpaper imitating the appearance of book-lined shelves offers the ideal solution. Providing an instantly weighty feel, the literary look helps to breathe life and interest into rooms that were previously arid and empty. Even minimalist spaces will benefit from the addition of a few worthy tomes, their linear appearance helping to deepen the desired effect of peace and tranquillity. Repro-book papers work well even in rooms not usually associated with studious calm: a wall of books in the kitchen makes a quirky contrast to domestic implements such as pots and pans, for example, while literary designs in the bathroom produce a similarly contradictory twist.

COPY-CAT PAPER

Gently ironic, wallpaper designs that imitate other papers are becoming increasingly popular in Western interiors thanks to our continued fascination with all things Zen. Taking inspiration from traditional shoji screens – a quintessential feature of Japanese interiors – the gridlike design of such papers mimics the calming symmetry of these age-old room dividers and bestow a similarly serene ambience. Available in calming neutrals, light, almost translucent shoji-style wallpaper is extremely versatile, working as well in large airy interiors as it does in smaller stuffier ones. In addition, the slightly raised effect of the gridwork creates an illusion of depth as well as providing textural interest.

The modern twist on imitation-paper patterns is manifested in superbly realistic designs that ape the appearance of used paper bags. Looking as though they have been roughly crumpled in order to create the apparently random wrinkles, the three-dimensional appearance of these wallpapers is actually the result of a painstaking and lengthy procedure. Best used in small rooms where their illusory effect will have the greatest impact, the appearance of crumpled papers is at once bizarre and strangely compelling.

Retro modern revival

NOSTALGIA

Reminiscent of times when life was slower and less complicated, nostalgia wallpaper is a fast and effective way to imbue interiors with a gentle sense of the past. The wide variety of old-fashioned motifs available – including seaside postcards, teacups, faded newsprint and Alpine lodges – enables the evocation of all kinds of different atmospheres. For example, papers depicting vintage kitchen utensils bring to mind the wholesome home-cooked food of the 1950s, while antique toiletries designs recall more elegant eras when cosmetics were decanted into silver-topped glass jars and dressing for dinner was de rigueur.

Not surprisingly, nostalgia papers depend on a palette of faded hues or washed-out monochrome in order to convey a sense of past times. This is

OPPOSITE The primary colours and blurred outlines of this modern cowboy design recall past times when life seemed simple and good.

RIGHT AND BELOW Nostalgic designs that depict antique toiletries have an enduring appeal, recalling the days when women always wore lipstick and men always shaved.

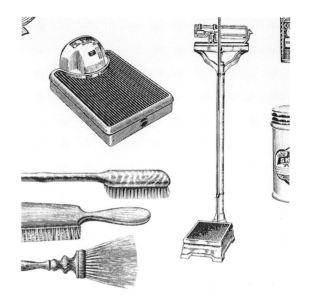

enhanced by motifs with slightly blurred outlines, which help to give an impression of bygone eras gradually becoming wreathed in the mists of time. But while the period look is at the heart of modern nostalgic wallpapers, their placement in the home is a much more straightforward affair thanks to the simplicity of the motifs. Thus papers depicting garden vegetables work best in a kitchen or larder, vintage toy designs in a children's playroom and hunting motifs in a stone-flagged hall.

Outdoor pursuits also provide a popular source of motifs for nostalgia-style papers. Papers printed with cowboys riding across the range, sailboats skimming across the sea and skiers slaloming down snowy mountains all evoke the simple pleasures of exercising in the open air. And, as befits their sense of energy and movement, these papers tend to have a bolder palette, with primary colours such as red, blue and green replacing the washed-out hues of static designs. Maximize their naive appeal by using them in activity areas such as bathrooms, passages and children's bedrooms or playrooms.

NEO-CLASSICAL

Although wallpaper was not notably popular when neo-classical style was at its height, the motifs associated with mid-eighteenth-century interiors look particularly good in clean contemporary spaces. For instance, a repetitive pattern of classical busts printed in silhouette has a crispness that is utterly modern, especially if you choose a design in graphic monochrome. Similarly, wreath motifs in gold or silver instil a clubby feel in studies or small sitting rooms, while the historical feel engendered by papers depicting Grecian vases or urns work best in light airy rooms where their graceful symmetry can be properly appreciated; papers depicting architectural features such as columns and pediments help to ground high-ceilinged rooms as well as give large rambling rooms a sense of cohesion and focus.

Covering your walls with faux-marble designs is another effective way to strike a neo-classical note. Papers range from flat expanses of colour threaded with just enough veining to give a feeling of depth and movement, to expensive hand-painted styles where the veining evolves across the paper in an apparently random manner, thus presenting a realistic imitation of real marble. Available in numerous colourways, faux-marble papers are hugely versatile, encompassing many different looks. Use pale colours to give a coolly minimalist effect, warmer shades to evoke feelings of grandeur, and darker styles to imbue rooms with a subtle sense of opulence. It should also be noted that not all marble designs strive for sophistication; instead, some are tinted with artificial hues including turquoise and shocking pink, and are ideal for giving interiors a colourful jolt of irony.

LEFT Wallpaper that features classical designs including statuary, sculpture, pottery and architectural elements such as friezes and pediments translates especially well in contemporary interiors thanks to its graphic appearance. Often rendered in black and white, the neo-classical look is particularly suited to interior spaces that have been rigorously stripped back, adding a sense a sense of drama without appearing too overpowering.

NEO-VICTORIAN

NEW-LOOK LACE

Often considered overly fussy, Victorian-style wallpaper has been stylishly reinterpreted to suit the less-is-more approach of contemporary interiors. A case in point is the new take on lace-effect designs, which enjoyed their heyday in nineteenth-century France, appearing as frou-frou confections of trompe l'oeil swags, ribbons and bows. Thankfully, contemporary lace wallpaper has been trimmed of its original details, eschewing the earlier extraneous details for designs that are both elegant and seductive.

To highlight its unique intricacy, lace wallpaper works best in small doses. To create a sensual boudoir effect, take inspiration from the film *Moulin Rouge* and paper one wall in a black delicately webbed design; then dress the bed with slippery satin sheets, pile a heap of velvet cushions on top and turn down

FAR LEFT The intricate cobwebby appearance of lace wallpaper is perfect for creating a vintage mood.

LEFT The gentle curves and pastel shades of this floral wallpaper create a feminine boudoir feel.

RIGHT Flocking is given a contemporary spin with a fresh palette of vivid colours. Team the paper with sleek, streamlined accessories for a striking textural contrast.

the lights. For vintage chic, complement a beautiful lace wall with antique furniture, brocade upholstery and a Venetian mirror. It is also possible to create a slick and sophisticated look by combining lace papers with furnishings in leather, latex and suede.

FUNKY FLOCK

At last, flocking has flung aside its dowdy image and reinvented itself as a funky modern wallcovering. Most often associated with the predominantly dark décor of Indian restaurants, the original palette of burgundy and grape has been replaced by acid-bright shades of turquoise, orange, scarlet and pink. For best results, use new-look flock in rooms that are large enough to withstand the dazzling textural onslaught. It is also possible to counter the deeply kitsch effect of flocked wallpaper with sleek mid-century-modern furnishings: a Panton chair in matt polypropylene or a Robin Day sofa will both lend instant gravitas, for example, as well as provide a smooth contrast to furry walls.

MODERN ANAGLYPTA

Extremely fashionable in Victorian times, Anaglypta wallpapers are currently enjoying a resurgence in popularity, thanks to their undeniably retro appearance. Formerly, Anaglypta was used to cover the space between the skirting (base) board and dado rail (positioned roughly at chair-back height). Its slightly raised surface was tough enough to withstand the inevitable wear and tear of scratches and bumps, and subsequently it was most often employed to cover the walls in transitional areas such as halls, passages and stairways.

The modern interpretation of Anaglypta gives this attractively textured paper the exposure it deserves. Currently used to cover entire walls, its three-dimensional appearance gives valuable depth and interest to contemporary interiors. Not only that, but Anaglypta also responds brilliantly to a variety of paint shades: use strong colours such as black, red or navy for a modern retro feel or paler shades to introduce a subtle sense of texture.

ART NOUVEAU AND ART DECO

The elegant and sophisticated design style known as Art Deco epitomizes the interwar years of the 1920s and 1930s. Art Deco originally developed in France between 1908 and 1912, and reached the height of its popularity in the years between 1925 and 1935. The term derives from the Exposition Internationale des Arts Décoratifs et Industriels Modernes – an influential design exhibition that was held in Paris in 1925.

Fundamentally, Art Deco grew out of – and was a reaction to – the French Art Nouveau style. Both had a decorative repertoire based on natural phenomena, but whereas Art Nouveau often featured exotic flowers and plants with twisting and climbing stems (scrolling acanthus leaves, thistle, poppy, wisteria and waterlily patterns were especially favoured), Art Deco employed a more restrained approach, depicting stylized floral arrangements such as roses or poppies grouped in bouquets or baskets. Marble, cloud or wave patterns were also fashionable.

In addition, many Art Deco papers showed highly mathematical forms, such as overlapping squares, oblongs, checks, cross-hatching and triangles. Bold outlines and strong colours were popular – especially shades of red, gold and brown – and different wallpaper designs were often combined in the same room. Also widely seen in the mid-1920s were pastel-coloured geometrics in which stripes, squares and triangles were harmoniously presented in subtly balanced tones of a single colour.

ABOVE Inspired by the naturalistic motifs of Art Nouveau, this Art Deco-style design has a more restrained approach, featuring static, highly stylized forms.

OPPOSITE Not for the faint-hearted, the flowing lines and rambling patterns of Art Nouveau-inspired designs are an exercise in bold spontaneity.

'I have made my world and it is a much better world than I ever saw outside.' LOUISE NEVELSON

OPPOSITE Dramatic advances in manufacturing inspired designers of the 1950s to create a plethora of machine-age motifs, which were, in turn, abstracted, as exemplified in this cleverly thought-out pattern with its technological feel.

LEFT Create a classic 1950s look with a backdrop of asymmetrical forms rendered in a bold palette of blue, yellow white and red-brown.

FABULOUS FIFTIES

Often referred to as mid-century modern, the 1950s look is much sought after in twenty-first-century interiors. In addition to streamlined furniture by the likes of Arne Jacobsen and Eero Saarinen, contemporary reinterpretations of retro wallpaper patterns are highly prized thanks to their graphic motifs and bright colours. The striking designs of the 1950s were the result of seismic technological, cultural and social changes: dramatic advances in manufacturing inspired a wealth of machine-age motifs, and cultural phenomena such as the fascination with outer space resulted in loopy atom-style patterns. The abstract paintings of artists such as Pablo Picasso, Paul Klee, Joan Miró and Henri Matisse supplied further inspiration, while a renewed zeal for strong colours – bright green, turquoise and yellow – was a reaction against the drabness of the war-torn 1940s.

For Scandinavian designers the 1950s were years of international triumph. Their output, which took the best of hand-crafted and machine approaches and blended them seamlessly, became synonymous with good taste and high quality, and resulted in wallpaper designs that depicted giant circles and wavy vertical bands displayed on rectangular grids. At the same time, the streamlined furniture designs that came out of America – often moulded from one of the new plastics – also influenced wallpaper design by introducing abstract asymmetrical forms that were reconfigured as stylized triangular or kidney patterns. Typical motifs of the time included cocktail glasses, harlequin figures, artist's palettes and guitars.

In terms of contemporary interiors, 1950s-inspired wallpaper works best when used with restraint. Cover one wall with a graphic design and team it with soft colours or white to keep the look simple and spacious. Alternatively, mix and match graphic wallpaper with soft furnishings upholstered in a similar style to create a medley of clashing prints.

SWINGING SIXTIES

Considering the variety of cultural influences that occurred during the 1960s, it is easy to see why this decade threw up so many design styles. There was art – first Pop with Andy Warhol and Roy Lichtenstein as its figureheads, then Op, led by Bridget Riley and her stripes. There was intergalactic travel, thanks to the NASA space programme. And there were drugs that gave users strange hallucinogenic visions. The 1960s also saw the eruption of youth culture as the baby-boom generation – born after the Second World War – came of age and demanded a new aesthetic identity. The result was a colourful and innovative visual idiom that continues to inspire contemporary wallpaper patterns to this day.

ABOVE Big florals inspired by the Art Nouveau movement, a signature feature of 1960s bold and brash wallpaper design, is re-created here.

MILLENNIAL FLOWER POWER

Lurid wallpaper featuring huge swirly flowers in clashing colours was a predominant design feature during the late 1960s and early 1970s. Inspired by drug-induced psychedelia, the hippie-trippy look is enjoying a revival in contemporary interiors owing to its enduring retro appeal. And while various modern interpretations include flowery designs in monochrome rather than clashing pinks and reds, rolls of the real thing – available in specialist wallpaper shops – are being snapped up by homeowners keen to emulate the punchy look of the century's most colourful and ebullient decade.

TOPICAL OP ART

Thanks to Bridget Riley's stripey canvasses wacky optical illusions were big news in the 1960s, inspiring wallpaper designers to inject a similar three-dimensional quality into their straight-up-and-down styles. An enthusiastic colourist, Riley presented vertical stripes in a mixture of candy blues, reds, greens, yellows and oranges, while her monochrome versions appeared to unfold magically into the distance. Reinterpretations of her work are just as effective at opening out space: use brilliantly striped papers in long dark hallways and graphic black-and-white styles in small rooms in need of an energy charge.

LEFT AND FAR LEFT These retro designs are reminiscent of the kaleidoscope patterns so popular in the 1960s, particularly towards the end of that decade when drug use inspired a wealth of hallucinogenic styles.

OPPOSITE Monochrome, favoured in fashionable 1960s interiors along with a palette of lurid colours, appears in this modern-day interpretation.

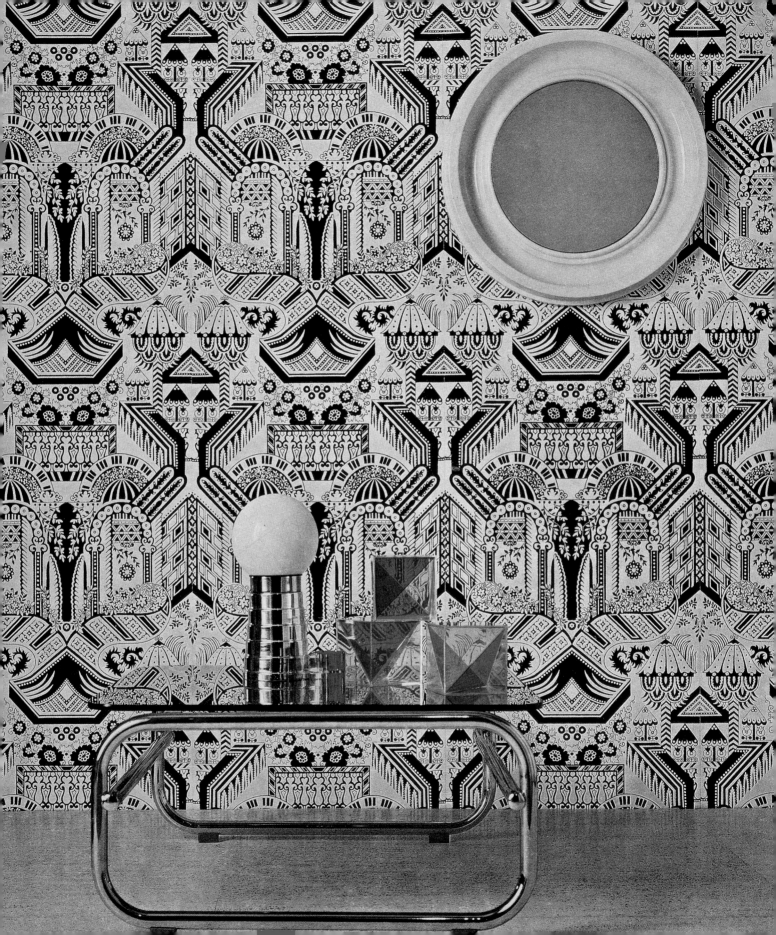

BAD-TASTE SEVENTIES

Derided by many as 'the decade that style forgot', the 1970s was deluged by an extraordinary range of aesthetic influences – from the tailend of pyschedelia, through the sparkle and shine of the glam-rock phenomenon, to the height of disco fever. Translated into domestic interiors, this cultural hotch-potch resulted in rooms with an eccentric edge and a visual vigour that inveterate retro freaks find irresistible.

Wallpaper was an important element in interior design during the 1970s. In a bid to keep pace with the deeply unsubtle furniture and furnishings – including brightly coloured floor cushions, bulky hi-fi systems, Oriental paper kites and fluorescent lava lamps – typical patterns featured geometric prints on a large scale. Vivid colours such as orange, purple and turquoise were favoured, in addition to an unshakeable (and contradictory) penchant for all shades of brown – from bitter chocolate to pasty beige. Horrifying tonal clashes were another feature of 1970s-style wallpaper – with combinations including orange and brown, orange and pink, purple and red, and pink and purple.

Picking out one or two walls in a contrasting colour or design was a quintessential 1970s touch. This approach also works well in contemporary interiors, especially if you combine stylized geometric patterns in pale fawn with walls painted baby blue or navy, for example. These alternative colour options of the 1970s palette are much less tiring on the eye yet still impeccably authentic.

OPPOSITE Gaudy wallpaper does not have to overwhelm. Instead, team lurid florals with tasteful furniture for a vigorous result.

RIGHT ABOVE AND BELOW Combine vivid designs with simple sleek furnishings to achieve a modern effect that is fresh and vibrant.

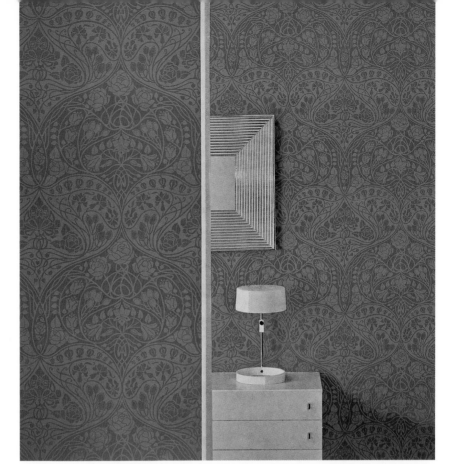

TWENTIETH-CENTURY KITSCH

ABOVE Modern papers printed with nostalgic motifs serve as gentle reminders that a good sense of style does not always have to be sophisticated.

There is nothing like a generous helping of kitsch to give your interiors a humorous lift. And the multitude of wallpaper designs produced over the past hundred years means there is a veritable treasure trove of patterns (available from retro wallpaper shops) just waiting to be discovered …

Choose from Disney designs featuring Dumbo, Mickey Mouse, Snow White and the Seven Dwarfs, or opt for other much-loved cartoon characters such as Fred and Barney from *The Flintstones*. Additional designs include Sindy, Barbie, Batman, Spiderman, James Bond, Luke Skywalker and the rest of the *Star Wars* cast.

SPORT

Wallpapers for sports fans range from football, hockey and baseball themes to signed portraits of star players. Alternatively, cover walls with images of skateboarders, snowboarders, skiers or surfers.

CRAZY FOR YOU

Animal lovers will go wild for wallpapers patterned with pets: favoured images are dogs – particularly Alsatians and Labradors – rabbits, cats and horses. Papers for popaholics variously depict David Cassidy, the Bay City Rollers, the Bee Gees and the Spice Girls, as well as many other stars from bygone eras.

'My image ... is a projection of everything that can be bought and sold, the practical but impermanent symbols that sustain us.'

ANDY WARHOL

LEFT The choice of wallpaper motifs is such that designers can choose from numerous wacky images: here, dental care takes centre stage.

BELOW Simple but iconic, the heart motif is a favourite image with teenage girls across the world. Choose scarlet for maximum impact.

Paper Art the big picture

BANNERS

Wallpaper hung as one vertical strip is an effective way to give interiors a splash of pattern and colour without committing to comprehensive coverage. Instead, banners make an arresting focal point, as they take on the prominence of a framed painting or drawing. In addition, because many contemporary wallpapers have such strong simple motifs, a single banner, made up of one or two drops of paper, is enough to make a powerful statement without appearing overly dominant. Choose from graphic images such as single-stem flowers, oversized feathers and large metallic circles on a matt background. Or, do an Andy Warhol and liven up your walls with images of everyday items such as knives, forks and spoons.

Although wallpaper designs are increasingly cutting-edge, the techniques used are often traditional. For example, the age-old method of screen-printing allows designers to produce small runs of exquisite handmade papers with a repeat that is so large it becomes almost unnoticeable. Screen-printing also enables a designer to print one oversized image to fill a single drop of paper, thus creating wallpaper that can be hung as an independent panel.

HANGING BANNERS

- Banners work best in minimalist rooms where they are the main focal point. Stick to neutral walls, wood floors and simple furnishings.
- Use banners to add a new aesthetic dimension. For example, three vertical strips will break up a large expanse of wall, while horizontal strips along the middle of a wall will help to counter high ceilings.
- The symmetry of banners reinforces a sense of ordered calm. Balance the linear look with contrasting pieces of curvilinear furniture.
- Always keep decoration in proportion with the scale of the room as banners in a small low-ceilinged room could make it feel more cramped.

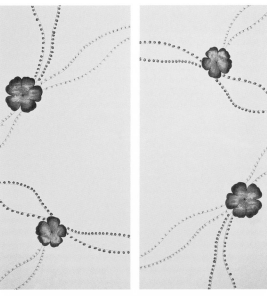

LEFT Matching panels are an effective way to decorate walls without committing to the full-on coverage of wallpaper.

OPPOSITE AND BELOW A banner creates a striking focal point without appearing too dominant. For maximum impact, choose single-stem flowers or feathers in jewel-bright shades.

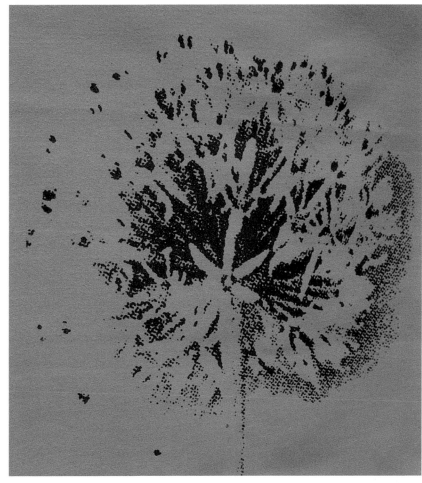

PANELS

For those of us who like the concept of wallpaper, but do not have the space – or nerve – to go for all-over coverage, a fibreboard panel plastered with a zany print is the ideal solution. An effective way to introduce controlled blocks of pattern into your rooms, papered panels create an arresting focal point with comparatively little effort or expense. Either propped up or hung directly on a wall like a picture, they cannot fail to electrify your space. Even diehard minimalists can get in on the act, using a single graphically patterned panel to emphasize the spartan simplicity of white walls and low-key furniture and furnishings.

Another advantage of using small sections of wallpaper in this way is that it allows you to introduce a truly showstopping print that would almost certainly seem over the top if applied extensively. Better still, if you get bored with one design, simply repaper your panel with an alternative pattern.

DECORATING WITH PANELS
- Use sections of colourful wallpaper to jazz up functional features such as headboards and screens used as room dividers.
- To create a funky patchwork effect, fix a variety of ready-made wallpaper panels on one wall in a medley of clashing designs.
- Mix horizontal and vertical panels across a room, combining them with painted areas of wall to produce linear and textural contrasts.
- Achieve striking optical effects by pasting different kinds of striped wallpaper on to panels and hanging them together on one wall.
- Visit vintage wallpaper shops to source some truly original designs. Often only available in one or two rolls, these papers are perfect if you want to cover just a small area.

ABOVE Brightly coloured banners work best in minimalist rooms where their image can be properly appreciated.

OPPOSITE Introduce blocks of pattern and colour into your interiors by covering boards with wacky wallpaper designs.

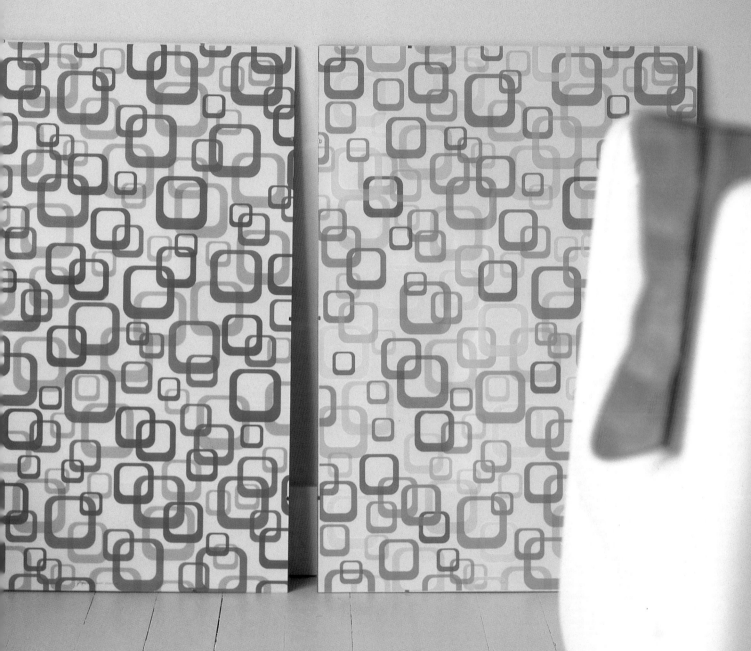

'There is no abstract art. You must always start with something. Afterward you can remove all traces of reality.' PABLO PICASSO

DIGITAL DESIGNS

As a result of digital technology, wallpaper patterns can be bigger, brighter and bolder than ever before. Computer-literate designers now have the tools to create images in amazingly vivid hues, and on a scale large enough to cover an entire wall with a single motif. Images can also be reduced, elongated or condensed, allowing designers the opportunity to invent wide variety of different looks at the touch of a button.

Manipulating an image on-screen throws up a very different challenge from creating a conventional wallpaper design, which depends on the more traditional skills of the artist – painting, drawing and interpretation. On a computer the imagination is freed by the technology – and the skill lies in the originality of the idea and the ability to exploit it as a concept. Designers working on-screen are also liberated from the constraints of the wallpaper repeat – the single most inhibiting factor in machine-produced wallpaper designs – and benefit from a preview of how the image would appear in situ.

WALL-SIZE FLORALS
Flower motifs are notably responsive to digital manipulation (see pages 29 and 53). For instance, if you enlarge a simple floral pattern to 20 times its original size, you will end up creating a design bordering on the abstract. Reduce the same design by a factor of 20, however, and you will be rewarded with a convoluted tangle of wiggles and dots.

Photographs of flowers also respond well to a spot of magnification – their leaves, petals and stamens revealing hitherto unseen details such as intricate veining, delicate mottling and bristling hairs.

OPPOSITE The vibrant colours and delicate structure of flowers are especially responsive to digital manipulation, giving an effect that is more painterly than photographic.

RIGHT For a totally dramatic effect, use a wall-sized floral in sparsely furnished rooms to re-create the hushed and peaceful ambience of an art gallery.

More painterly than photographic, the triffidlike appearance of wall-size florals is becoming increasingly popular in locations such as bars, restaurants and hotels where there is enough space to accommodate the impact. That said, it is perfectly feasible to paste motifs, throbbing with colour, on the walls of your home. Large rooms with high ceilings offer the best setting, and furniture and furnishings should be kept to the bare minimum in order to create the unintrusive ambience of a contemporary art gallery.

These days it is also possible to customize digital images to suit your surroundings. As a rising number of designers, wallpaper manufacturers and photographic shops produce bespoke prints, which can be scaled up to fit any wall, the only limits are your imagination and your budget, as these new specialist printing techniques are extremely costly. A less expensive but equally innovative option is to cover walls with photocopies. Simply choose a black-and-white photograph, or even an image from a book, have it blown up at a photocopy shop and then paste it on the wall. Alternatively, take lots of smaller copies of the same image and paste them on to walls to form a repetitive pattern.

'Art does not reproduce what we see.
It makes us see.' PAUL KLEE

OPPOSITE Photomurals are perfect for giving interiors an extra dimension.

RIGHT The Manhattan skyline provides a glittery backdrop to the shiny décor of this pink and silver bedroom.

BELOW Different images pasted together create a striking mural effect.

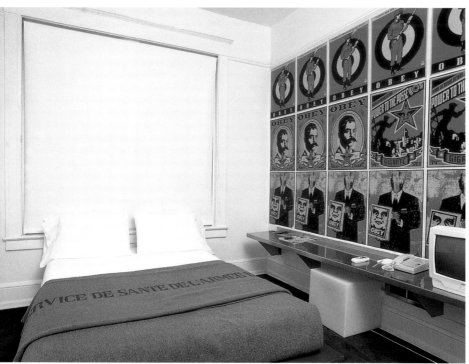

PHOTOMURALS

In the 1940s fine art exerted a strong influence on wallpapers, with manufacturers offering screen-printed murals by artists such as Henri Matisse, Joan Miró and Raphael, including the latter's decorations for the Loggia of the Vatican. Mural wallpaper, which became popular in the early nineteenth century, has largely survived to this day, but there have been some significant changes in style and content that reflect the developments in both urban and rural life, as well as in printing technology. For example, in America during the 1950s and 1960s fashionable photomurals showed subjects as diverse as the New York skyline, groups of commuting office workers and Highway 66 winding its way through its desert landscape. Similarly, the Pop Art and Op Art of the 1960s was readily translated to visually dramatic pictorial papers.

Murals are fast regaining popularity in many contemporary homes due to our continuing desire to establish a connection with the great outdoors. Providing the perfect complement to natural-fibre flooring and wood furnishings, photomurals

depicting panoramic vistas such as tropical beach scenes, autumnal forests, gushing waterfalls and even golf courses are breathtaking ways of bringing the outside in. In addition, these giant posters, so often dismissed as little more than kitsch novelties, are actually extremely effective at giving rooms a new aesthetic dimension. For instance, use mountainous scenes to add grandeur and height to low-ceilinged rooms, sun-filled meadows to introduce a sense of light and space in poky areas, and beach scenes where sea and sky merge on the horizon to strengthen the relaxing ambience of minimalist bathrooms.

The twenty-first century successor to the photomural, however, is sure to be the hologram projection. The scope is huge. All you need to cover your wall with a larger-than-life image is a projector and your favourite photograph captured on transparency. You could project stylish black-and-white prints in your living areas, or soothing pictures of flower-filled fields in your bedroom. Moreover, because the images are transient, it is possible to change the look or mood of a room in an instant.

NURSERY PAPERS

Wallpapers for nurseries were produced in increasing quantities in the latter part of the twentieth century. Many were photogravure murals designed to cover flush doors in a child's bedroom. While some of the original subjects, such as the tales of Beatrix Potter, Thomas the Tank Engine and Mickey Mouse, are still popular today, the genre has constantly accommodated new characters including the Power Rangers, the Simpsons and Harry Potter.

OPPOSITE AND LEFT White beaches and lush coconut palms set against an azure sky give interiors a perennial exoticism, while lakes and mountain scenes introduce a breath of fresh air.

BELOW Horses galloping through the surf bring a wonderful feeling of energy and movement to this narrow corridor.

'The big artist ... keeps an eye on Nature and steals her tools.' THOMAS EASKINS

Wall finishes

Paint funky strokes

MANIPULATING SPACE

The popularity of paint as a decorating material is easy to understand. Inexpensive and widely available in a vast choice of colours and finishes, paint is easy to use, simple to change and capable of transforming interiors fast and effectively. It can also be used to manipulate space – helping to highlight the good points of a room and disguise the less positive ones. In particular, bright colour draws the eye to the part of the room where you want to focus attention, or alternatively divert the gaze.

For instance, paint one end of a long narrow room in a vibrant shade, both to make the room seem as wide as possible (you can also take the colour round to adjacent walls) and to draw the end wall forward. Or 'hide' an unattractive fireplace that you cannot remove by painting it the same colour as the wall. It is also possible to draw attention to interesting architectural elements in a room by emphasizing them

with a bright splash of emulsion (latex): paint a curved wall in a sumptuous shade to accentuate its sensuous form, for example, or highlight an arched doorway by painting the frame in a jewel-bright hue.

A spot of nifty brushwork also helps to correct the appearance of structural elements that may be less than perfect. For example, low-ceilinged rooms will benefit from any kind of décor that gives an illusion of height. Try painting wide vertical stripes on the walls, keeping colours light. To combat the claustrophobia that thin rooms may induce, make space feel squarer and less corridorlike by visually lowering the ceiling. To achieve this, paint the walls to three-quarter height in one colour, then do the last quarter in white to reflect light. Conversely, make lofty rooms appear less lanky by painting the ceiling in a dark colour, and use light cool shades below to draw the eye to the lower part of the room.

FASHIONABLE FINISHES

As an ever-growing number of fashion designers launch homeware ranges, the link between sartorial chic and interior style is becoming increasingly apparent. These days when the fashion press dubs grey or brown the 'new black', it is not long before seductive shades of these colours are on sale in the form of deeply covetable cushions, china, fabric and … paint.

It is not just trendy hues that are influencing interior schemes, however. Paints that mimic fashionable fabrics are also popular – with denim-effect emulsion coming top of the class for its casual utilitarian appeal. Jeans-style paint has a slightly gritty texture, which can be applied to give a variety of stylish looks: if you want to achieve the pristine appearance of indigo denim, for example, simply use paint straight from the can and leave to dry. For a more distressed effect, drag a comb in both vertical and horizontal directions to create a worn look that imitates the warp and weft of the fabric. And remember, denim walls do not have to be rendered in blue to look impressive: try red, black or brown for an off-the-wall effect.

Paint that imitates the appearance of corduroy is also hip, thanks to its current renaissance in the fashion stakes. Available in a variety of shades – from tan to violet – this paint is even grittier than denim emulsion (latex). To get the best effect, roller it on over a similarly coloured base, then brush over the wet paint with a stiff short-bristled brush to produce a finely grooved look.

DOS AND DON'TS WITH PAINT COLOUR

- Choose 'natural' paint colours that look as if they have always been in situ. Any colour can work in any room, so long as the tone is right.
- Introducing colour doesn't have to mean painting walls in strong reds and yellows. With pale colours and neutrals (even white), just remember to pick a warm tone.
- Ignore colour trends: opt for shades that attract you and that you know you can live with.
- When selecting your paint, just remember that the most important thing is that your choice of colour fits the concept of the room.
- If you're scared of colour, use it in a small area – an alcove or washroom, for example – until you get used to it. Sometimes you have to paint a whole wall or room in a particular colour to see if you like the effect. In this case, keep ceilings white so the eye has something to rest on when it tires, or keep walls white and contrast them with a strongly coloured ceiling.

GLITTER AND METALLIC

Coveted by schoolgirls and style gurus alike, the new raft of glitter paints give walls an instantly glamorous sheen. Easy to apply – you use them as a top coat on an already painted wall – these paints contain flakes suspended in a mixture that permits the application of a thin and even spread of glitter with each brushstroke. In addition, depending on the size of the flakes (paints with either big or tiny glitter particles are available), it is possible to create as dramatic or as subtle an effect as you want. Sold in myriad different colours, the appearance of glitter paint is also affected by the background colour of the wall. For example, if you want to create a stardust effect, apply glitter paint over a dark shade for a celestial look that works spectacularly well on ceilings. Alternatively, apply glitter paint on to a pale surface for a subtle ethereal look, which will shimmer and glisten as light plays across the surface.

FAST FINISHES

One of the most appealing aspects of paint is its ability to give fast effective results. Better still, advanced techniques mean that it is now possible to achieve all sorts of stunning paint effects through the use of simple kits. A good example is crackle-effect paint, which is supplied in two spray cans – one containing the basecoat and the other to give the crackled top coat. A far cry from the days when a crackle effect had to be painstakingly rendered, this method requires little or no expertise. All you have to do is

OPPOSITE Use white paint in rooms where the walls are flooded with sunlight in order to maximize the shadows created by coloured glassware.

RIGHT Painted metallic stripes in delicate pastel hues give walls a glamorous sheen as well as adding a dash of sartorial chic.

spray the paint, bearing in mind that the thicker the base coat, the larger the cracks in the top coat will appear. Use tan and brown to create a dramatically graphic effect or monochrome to give a gritty urban note; for a stone-flecked appearance, spray two coats from the top-coat can to create an illusion of solidity. It is also possible to fashion convincing stone-effect walls – including granite and marble – using similar spray-on formulas.

The new generation of paints also encompasses lustrous emulsions with a pearly or metallic finish. More expensive than plain pigments – and available in neutrals and pale cool tones as well as bronze and gold – these paints give a luxe opulent look and work best when applied in small doses. A good place to use them is on a wall opposite a door, or surrounding a fireplace so that their reflective qualities are fully exploited. Metallic paint is also great for funking up domestic areas, as its shimmery glamour counters the workaday feel of kitchens, studies or larders. Pearlized paint is perfect for adding style, luxury and a subtle touch of femininity to any corner of your home. Use it in a bedroom to soften edges and instil a harmonious mood, in a living area to evoke a feeling of elegant grandeur, and in a bathroom to enhance a sense of pristine cleanliness.

'I try to apply colours like words that shape poems, like notes that shape music.'

JOAN MIRÓ

NOVELTY FINISHES

These days not only has the choice of paint colours increased at a spanking rate but the variety of novelty paints is also on the up: choose from magnetic or glow-in-the-dark styles or cover your walls with scented paint, which comes in a feast of delicious flavours such as watermelon, orange and raspberry. Originally incorporated to make painting fun for children, and to mask the chemical smell, the scent in these formulations fades after application, although research into the creation of permanent-aroma paints is ongoing.

BLACKBOARD PAINT

Another winner in the instant-gratification stakes is blackboard paint. Not only does it provide an extra novelty in children's playrooms but it is also ideal for areas such as kitchens and halls where you might want to scribble the odd recipe or jot down telephone messages. The flat matt appearance of blackboard paint looks good when applied in bold graphic patterns – instead of the classic square or rectangle, try a large circle in the centre of a white wall. Even better, it is also possible to eschew the traditional black finish for colours such as pillarbox red, royal blue, and olive green. With such groovy shades available, how will you be able to resist the opportunity to indulge in a few artistic doodles?

LIGHTING TRICKS

If you are someone who quickly tires of your décor, you can alter the colour of your interior by the skilful deployment of light. To do this, paint walls white and then install hidden bulbs that will wash them with shades of blue, yellow or pink at the setting of a switch. In addition, fabulous effects such as iridescence and strobe are now attainable, with the inclusion in the paint of tiny particles that affect the way light plays on it.

OPPOSITE Blackboard paint is available in a number of different colours including blue, scarlet and olive green.

LEFT AND BELOW Functional and aesthetic, blackboard paint works well in kitchens where it can be used to jot down messages or recipes.

MODERN PAINT EFFECTS

Due to their unfortunate association with pastel shades and fussy 1980s style 'paint effects' are often dismissed as being devoid of style. And while there is more than a grain of truth in this with regards to rag-rolling and stippling, it certainly does not apply to contemporary paint effects, which simulate a variety of finishes including leather, silk, rubber and blended neon in strong bright colours.

One of the very best examples of modern wall treatments is spattering, a technique that gives walls an edgy Jackson Pollock effect. Put simply, spattering is the flicking of paint – usually two or three colours – on to a surface to produce small but varied spots. To achieve this, a paint brush is loaded with diluted water-based paint and the handle tapped with a stick to propel the paint in a random but not uncontrolled manner on to the surface of the wall. The palette can be varying tones of the same hue, or similar tones of different colours with perhaps one that is brighter

RIGHT Stencil designs of glamorous stilettos give this dressing room a fashionable kick.

LEFT Peacock feathers in pastel shades have a graceful delicacy, and complement the opulence of the chair.

FAR LEFT These single-rose motifs are typical of modern stencil designs, which are much bolder and more immediate than their predecessors.

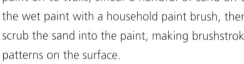

to lift the other colours. The beauty of spattering lies in its versatility: you can make larger spots and dribbles by standing back from walls and flicking the paint more forcefully, or a densely packed stone effect by spattering earth-coloured paint from close-up.

Combing is another technique that has been updated to create a more decorative look. Originally designed to give a simple woodgrain effect, this simple method is now being used to produce patterns ranging from simple trellis or cane effects to graphic three-dimensional tartans. It is also possible to use a comb like a calligraphy pen and draw fluid swirly designs through bright patches of wet paint to create a sense of fluid modernity. Alternatively, give your walls authentic texture by applying a sand-effect treatment. Simply roller

paint on to walls, smear a handful of sand on to the wet paint with a household paint brush, then scrub the sand into the paint, making brushstroke patterns on the surface.

STENCILLING

Stencilling is a versatile and attractive way to introduce colour and pattern to walls. In recent years, however, this fast and effective decorating device has acquired a rather drab image due to a plethora of patterns featuring lacklustre florals and limp trailing foliage. Thankfully, contemporary stencils are bolder, brighter and more immediate than in their previous incarnation. Choose from a wide range of manufactured designs, or make your own from pieces of thin cardboard or acetate.

PAINT ART

USING PAINT IN 'NEUTRAL' INTERIORS

It is entirely feasible to introduce bright paint shades into neutral interiors without compromising the tasteful low-key effect. One option is to apply a vibrant paint shade on a single wall only – with a coat of white paint underneath to increase the brightness of colour. Another idea is to put paint on just a section of wall – behind a sofa, say, or at the head of a bed – to create a focus and highlight that particular piece of furniture. Alternatively, paint coloured circles, squares or rectangles on to a wall to create a funky graphic effect and accentuate the clean lines of minimalist design.

Another way to create a subtle sense of variety while retaining a sense of spaciousness is to apply

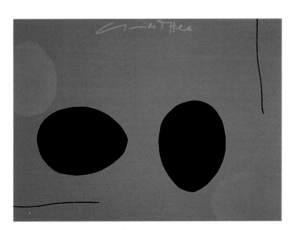

ABOVE The delicate appearance of this Japanese-style panel, set at the head of the bed, acts as a calming focal point in this pared-down room.

LEFT Walls painted with graphic shapes provide the perfect complement to the stark lines of modern décor, and harmonize with the minimalist theme.

OPPOSITE Most effective in large interiors, painted murals can have a huge impact. For best results, stick to a pastel palette and a simple theme.

identical paint shades in different finishes such as matt, silk and gloss. This allows you to paint patterns, or even words, on the walls without the overall effect appearing too obvious. The patterns could be in the form of spheres (large or small, in lines or dotted randomly) or stripes painted in horizontal or vertical configurations. If you are looking for a quick and easy result, choose large and bold areas of the different finishes, so there is less work involved in the preparation (achieved either by fine-lining designs with a paintbrush or using masking tape to delineate different areas). Another option is to use very slight variations in colour tones to produce the same effect.

MURALS

From ancient times, artists have applied paint to walls to create imaginary scenes that can transport the viewer into a dream landscape. Popular vistas have included the Italian lakes, a flower-filled meadow with distant snow-capped peaks or an idyllic island surrounded by the calming depths of an azure sea.

politick will rule in a surfers' world.

Fabric touchy, feely

FABRIC COVERINGS

Covering the walls of a room with fabric has long been a popular interior-decorating device – providing a three-dimensional feel that neither wallpaper nor paint can achieve. From the fourteenth century onwards, woven tapestries were frequently used as wallhangings, and by the seventeenth century fabric hangings, including velvet and wool moquette, were introduced, their warm and enveloping properties interchanged with cooler and lighter ones of taffeta and silk in the summer months. During the nineteenth century fabric was either hung flat, in rectangular folds or deep festoons to create a dramatic, billowing display, or it was hung from poles fixed on to walls to create an all-round curtain effect.

The appeal of fabric-covered walls endures to this day, although the contemporary taste for minimalist furnishings calls for a more restrained approach. Fabric is usually lined and attached to walls with glue, tacks or double-sided tape. Alternatively, fabric-faced wallpaper can be used to achieve a flatter, leaner look. Covering walls with fabric provides the ultimate solution to the problem of hiding imperfections – and the variety of styles to choose from is huge.

In minimalist interiors fabric wallcoverings are an effective way to bestow density and texture. Neutral-coloured materials such as hessian, linen or grasscloth are superbly suited to softening the hard edges of minimalist bedrooms – as well as adding a textured sensuality to stark spaces – while luxurious fabrics such as velvets, damasks and chiffons create a sense of opulence. At the other end of the textural spectrum, exquisite laces and embroidered gossamer silks evoke a romantic atmosphere. In contrast, the new breed of synthetic textiles – ranging from translucent polypropylene stretched taut on frames to Japanese polyester fabrics woven with aluminium or copper – inject a funky modern feel.

CLASSIC

Strong, supple and sophisticated, leather is staging a serious comeback in contemporary interiors. Used for floors as well as furniture such as tables and consoles, it is also making its mark as a modern wallcovering, providing a versatile alternative to more conventional cladding. Wonderfully tactile, as well as chic, durable and functional, leather walls offer brilliantly effective insulation from cold and noise. Better still, modern pressing methods continue to improve on nature's work so that contemporary leathers are stain-, light- and moisture-proof as never before.

Available in tiles or wall-size panels, the only drawback of leather is the expense. The good news, however, is that a little goes a long way, allowing for the creation of a variety of looks without breaking the bank. Cover a study alcove to mimic the sombre appearance of a gentleman's club, for example, or clad the wall behind a bed with a glove-soft style to evoke the old-fashioned gentility of a first-class cabin. Alternatively, use overstitched tiles in a range of colours such as brown, mustard, sage, cherry and taupe to conjure up a 1970s patchwork effect, or go for the surprise factor and decorate walls with a shocking-pink plaited style. An additional advantage of leather is its compatibility with other natural materials. Combine it with wood for a rugged yet sophisticated look, stone for a grand and monumental impression, or extravagant fabrics for a look that is utterly sensuous.

GLAMOROUS

Fabric wallcoverings work best when they are used to create a dramatic and theatrical sense of opulence. Cherished by affluent homeowners during the seventeenth and eighteenth centuries, the extravagant appearance of walls lined with sumptuous materials such as velvet, devoré, silk,

ABOVE For a supersybaritic look, combine padded walls with silk bedlinen.

OPPOSITE The sumptuous appearance of padded satin walls is highlighted by an eclectic mix of furniture and furnishings that help to create a truly flamboyant effect.

satin and damask is enjoying a renaissance as the vogue for unusual wallcoverings gathers momentum.

The rich variety of silk fabrics available facilitates the creation of many different looks – all oozing splendour. For a louche intimate feel, swathe walls in velvet and go for unexpected colours – deep purple or raspberry pink, for instance – to add an extra frisson. Bold modern colours also work well with other traditional fabrics such as taffeta or moiré; choose cerulean, lime green or tangerine orange to pump up the pace.

The latest traditional fabric to be given a new twist is damask. Its subtly interwoven patterns look great when juxtaposed with the clean lines of modern furniture, and its striking appearance fits with the bold direction of twenty-first-century interiors. For an elegantly classical look, line walls with damask in forest green or deep aubergine; alternatively, use soft shades of khaki or Parma violet to create a relaxed mood. Flocking has also come into its own of late (see page 83); available in acid-bright hues or trendy matt black, it can be combined with polished aluminium for a dramatic textural contrast, or with polystyrene wall tiles, which will reinforce its fundamentally kitsch appeal.

For full-on glamour, silk wallcoverings are the way to go. Button-quilted versions will evoke the lush old-fashioned style of nineteenth-century bedrooms, while padded satin gives a Hollywood starlet look. Colours should be showy: gold, silver, bronze, pink and red will all do the trick, while bright shiny white is the perfect choice for wannabe divas.

FASHIONABLE

Although there is a wide selection of wallpapers imitating the appearance of trendy threads, nothing beats the real thing. From emerald astrakhan or fuchsia corduroy to saris glittering with mirrorwork, the only limits are your imagination and your nerve. Even fake fur is a candidate, proving to be as exotic

LEFT White leather wallcoverings give a 1960s space-age feel.

RIGHT ABOVE Supple suede is the ultimate in luxury wallcoverings.

RIGHT BELOW Combine fur-covered walls with metal furnishings to create textural contrast.

today as real fur was when twentieth-century style luminaries Cecil Beaton and Diana Vreeland used animal pelts to decorate their homes. To introduce fur into your home, simply attach skins – from long-haired goat to shorn sheep's hide – to walls with strong double-sided carpet tape. In addition, the modern troglodyte look presents numerous design options: combine with organic wood furnishings for a rustic log-cabin style, or team fluffy blond fur with black leather for a dash of 007 glamour.

Floaty fabrics imbue interiors with a light, spiritual. Use antique white lace behind a bed for romance, pastel chiffon to effect a fey arty ambience, or layered gossamer panels for veiled mystery. Another idea is to dye flimsy fabrics in brilliant hues to create a pleasing juxtaposition of delicate texture with bold colour. The detailed patterning on net curtains makes them gorgeous wallhangings, whether dyed in pale pastel shades or trippy fluorescent ones.

The fashionable appeal of the retro home – which has borrowed heavily from the 1960s and 1970s – has brought synthetic furnishings and fittings to the fore. Part Pop, part kitsch, this trend has seen the re-emergence of classic fabrics such as Astroturf and PVC – both of which make superb wallcoverings when used unexpectedly. Clad kitchen walls with fake grass or use PVC to funk up 'serious' spaces such as studies or dining areas.

NATURAL

Adding instant texture to walls, natural fabrics also provide more insulation than paper. Woollen felt, made by pressing and injecting wool with steam, is one of the most eco-friendly of wallcoverings, giving a fabulously tactile background without being intrusive. Available in jewel-bright hues as well as muted shades including chocolate brown and battleship grey, felt is also superbly versatile, imparting warmth to draughty corridors, softness to children's playrooms and intimacy to cosy dens.

OLD AND NEW WALLHANGINGS

The term 'wallhanging' tends to conjure up images of fusty medieval tapestries depicting scenes of long-forgotten battles. But modern versions are a far cry from the ornate embroidered hangings that were status symbols centuries ago. These days textiles on walls perform the same function as paintings and photographs, acting as changeable art that can soften the occasional hard edge of modern décor.

Contemporary homeowners can also afford to be more flexible in their display of antique weavings, which were originally crafted for a particular purpose. These days, instead of using prayer rugs for kneeling on, we can hang them on the wall or mount them behind a pane of Perspex. The appeal of vintage wallhangings lies in their exotic designs and jewel-bright hues: an antique throw, framed and hung on a wall, can instantly lift the energy of a room, while a timeworn paisley shawl or hand-stitched quilt both provide dramatic focal points.

For individuality, create your own wallhanging. A framed silk scarf, or a series of framed fabric pieces, can both look very striking, for example. You can also try displaying strips of material cut into unusual shapes – long and thin, for example, to emphasize narrow walls; alternatively, delineate space with a Chinese silk runner, an elegant length of lace or a bolt of brilliant brocade. Strong large-scale patterns like plaids, stripes and dots make a bold statement, while ethnic textiles add exoticism to Western interiors. Hang Indonesian batiks for a clean monochrome look, florid Moroccan embroideries for casbah cool or Peruvian ikat weaves for vivid intricacy.

Brightly patterned rugs are another option. Providing the perfect foil to neutral room schemes, types range from Oriental carpets to Persian kelims and South American mats in brilliant reds, pinks and turquoise. Ultra-modern compositions include

abstract styles, graphic Op Art patterns and designs interwoven with sheet metal, Perspex and chainmail.

HANGING RUGS
- Use decorative patterns to give energy to lifeless spaces such as a spartan hallway.
- Choose a pattern for the impact it will have in its intended hanging space – not because you find the colour or design generally appealing.
- Look to foreign cultures for inspiration: ethnic weaves add warmth and texture and provide the perfect complement to pared-down interiors.
- Mix rugs and textiles from different cultures: a Navajo blanket with a Turkish kelim, for example.
- Remember that rugs are not just rectangular or square. Carpetmakers are creating unusual morphic and flowing shapes, so think about which shape best suits your space.

ABOVE A simple cloth wall banner provides a graphic focal point in an otherwise austere interior.

OPPOSITE Fabric cut into individual squares and pasted on to thin board makes an arresting decorative feature.

Tiles cool coverage

CERAMIC TILES

The simple ceramic tile – a small piece of fired clay that has been embellished or left plain – is a magical decorating device that has been used throughout the ages to enhance, emphasize and transform both the interiors and exteriors of buildings. Today ceramic tiles continue to be a popular decorative feature and can be used in a variety of different ways to clad almost every room in the home. Luckily, tiles are fairly easy to put up, and can be applied to almost all wall finishes including paint, paper, brickwork, plaster and plasterboard, and even existing tiles.

Durable, water-resistant and easy to keep clean, ceramic tiles have regular dimensions that give a pleasing rhythm to interior spaces, helping to complement the clean lines of modern design. One of the most recent trends in tiled decoration is a panel or mural that has been custom designed. There are many ceramic artists who will take on special commissions for anything from a panel of four or six tiles to a mural that covers yards and yards of wall.

It is important to remember that tiles should be applied with a wholehearted approach, as decorative squares that have been restricted to meagre splashbacks behind kitchen or bathroom sinks, or relegated to a stingy border running around the edge of the bath, can look a tad dreary. Tiling that ends at an indeterminate place midway up a wall always looks unconvincing, whereas whole-tiled rooms appear confident and striking.

Ceramic tiles are available in an enormous variety of colours, textures, patterns and finishes. Ranging from cheap to extremely expensive, styles on offer include elegant octagonals in brilliant colours or simple squares featuring snazzy relief designs or pictorial motifs. Smooth metallics and elegant mother-of-pearl finishes are also available. Retro designs such as tiles in the shape of bevelled bricks or wedge shapes (which give the higgledy-piggledy impression of children's building blocks) look particularly chic in contemporary interiors – as do hand-painted tiles, which are enjoying a huge resurgence in popularity.

DIGITAL TILES

Most exciting of all, however, is the advent of the digitally designed tile, which has turned traditional methods of production on its head. Using photographic images that have been scanned into a computer and enhanced before being transferred to tiles, modern motifs include crisp Op Art geometrics and striking surreal ones, as well as hyper-realistic fruit, vegetables and flowers; you can even get an abstracted version of the London Underground map. The only disadvantage of these colourful tiles is the expense: digital designs are not for the cash-strapped.

OPPOSITE AND LEFT The new generation of ceramic tiles includes a wealth of psychedelic designs that have been digitally printed to produce patterns that are brighter, bolder and more zany than before. Ranging from modern-retro styles to marble-effect ones – and available in acid-bright shades of pink, purple and green – these new-look wallcoverings are guaranteed to pump up the pace in modern interiors.

look or cobbled tiles to create a kitsch fairytale appearance. An elegantly classical note can be struck with marble tiles, which, owing to modern technology, are now thinner, lighter and less expensive than before. Choose from pure white Carrara to tiles in a selection of hues, including green, pink, red, brown, gold and black.

BRICK AND SLATE

Brick walls are also hip in contemporary interiors, thanks to the fashion for loft-style apartments where exposed surfaces are all the rage. As a result, the formerly traditional profile of brick has become rather more cutting-edge – its interesting textural surface giving warmth and depth to both rustic and urban settings. Nonstructural applications involve the use of thin brick 'slips', which are cemented to walls in standard brick-bond fashion. As with many other forms of wall cladding, this is not a job lightly undertaken, although the end more than justifies the means as the 'honest' appearance of this material infuses interiors with a sense of authenticity. There many styles of brick cladding to choose from, Use long narrow brick tiles for a tasteful elegant look or mix quirky relief styles with plain plasterwork to create textural contrast.

Slate is one of the most versatile of all stones and is excellent for wall cladding, as it is easily split into thin tiles. Durable and waterproof, it is also cheaper than granite, marble and limestone. Typical colours include sombre hues of blue-grey, blue-black and grey-green. Most types have a sleek wet appearance due to their mica content, and this makes them the perfect for cladding walls in minimalist interiors where the look is stark and clean. For a rougher, more rustic effect, use riven slate (tiles that have been split rather than sawn), which has an attractive and irregular appeal.

STONE

ABOVE Ceramic tiles designed to create an uneven surface offer a contemporary and unusual alternative to the standard flat variety, giving a three-dimensional effect that, in turn, casts interesting shadows.

Capable of appearing coolly inviting or warm and earthy, stone is fast becoming a quintessential feature in contemporary interiors thanks to the enduring trend for natural furnishings. In addition to stone floor pavers, stone wall tiles are sought after, offering the kind of elemental simplicity that modern homes demand. For most interior surfaces, stone tiles measuring up to 1.5 cm (½ in) in thickness can simply be fixed directly to the wall using adhesive. While larger tiles increase a sense of monumentality and work best in rooms with grand proportions, small tiles look most effective in less spacious areas.

The main advantage of stone is its aesthetic variation. Available in a stunning multiplicity of colours, patterns and finishes, it enables the creation of numerous different looks – from cool limestone to boldly flecked granite. Use irregularly shaped blocks of fieldstone to give a modern-rustic

dyes, which soften the harsh effect, and the addition of resin produces an exceptionally smooth and glossy finish. In addition, a photo-etching technique has recently been developed, which allows images and graphics to be transferred on to concrete tiles. Admittedly, such customized designs are expensive, but the advent of this new technology serves to highlight the exciting potential of this much-maligned material.

LEFT A cross-section of a hyper-realistic cabbage turns traditional kitchen tile design on its head, and looks especially striking in minimalist surroundings.

BELOW Eschewing itsy-bitsy motifs for outsize ones, modern tile designs feature images such as this enlarged shell, which dominates the interior of a shower cubicle.

CONCRETE

Often viewed as brutal and unforgiving, concrete is gaining credibility in the domestic arena thanks to a number of modern designers who have highlighted its sensuous appeal. Without doubt, exposed concrete walls present a bold and uncompromising approach to interior design, but the overall effect does not have to appear avant-garde. Instead, concrete can be used to give an urban-naturelle look that is both textural and dramatic.

Applied in the form of panels or tiles – and much less expensive than stone – the rugged surface of unfinished concrete provides an effective contrast to smoother materials such as metal and glass, and is particularly successful in minimalist interiors where the furnishings have been ruthlessly stripped back.

The image of concrete as a utilitarian material is belied by the range of colours and finishes available, including acid-etched, polished and sealed with acrylic. Colour is created through the use of brilliant

MOSAIC

The ideal wallcovering for confined areas like shower cubicles and washrooms is mosaic – tiling at its tiniest. Made from a variety of materials including ceramic, marble, stone, terracotta and vitreous glass, mosaic can appear to shimmer with colour, helping to imbue walls with depth and dimension. Dating back 5,000 years, mosaic was used by the Romans and the Egyptians to decorate the walls and floors of their residences, but the peak of mosaic artistry was achieved by the Byzantines, whose skill was such that solid walls seemed to dematerialize into a mass of complex pattern.

These days it is possible to replicate the intricate beauty and heightened sense of mysticism of antique designs by employing a skilled mosaicist. Less complicated designs, which can still look highly sophisticated, can be accomplished with a little basic training, while those with no skill whatsoever can resort to mosaic tiling in sheet form, which enables surfaces to be covered quickly and easily. Available backed either with netting or with a peel-off paper, mosaic in this last format generally comprises a single solid colour or a random arrangement of different shades. Both make striking contemporary backgrounds for bathrooms and kitchens.

METAL TILES

The versatility of the metal aesthetic provides a wide choice of wallcoverings, which look especially stunning in hi-tech kitchens. Choose from brushed-steel tiles to create a soft-look wallcovering or high-shine versions that give a modern cutting-edge effect. Other available alternatives include lightweight aluminium, tin, white metal, soft, malleable zinc and warm-toned copper that can be brushed and patinated to create a reflective surface.

MIRRORED TILES

Another funky option is to use mirrored tiles on walls. Reminiscent of the 1970s when twinkly, sparkly surfaces were all the rage, these reflective squares of light are a great way to add pizzazz to plasterwork, as well as helping to multiply interior views. Mirror tiles are sold in a wide selection of sizes, ranging from large uninterrupted expanses which create a sense of stylish elegance, to smaller mosaic styles that give a retro disco look.

OPPOSITE Shiny aluminium tiles that have a rippled surface create an interesting juxtaposition with unvarnished wood walls.

ABOVE A metal curtain picks up the industrial theme featured on a series of photographic wall tiles – and completes the edgy urban look.

CORK AND WOOD

The butt of many an interior designer's joke, cork tiles now top the shopping list of environmentally aware, style-conscious consumers. Brilliant for sound and heat insulation, this 1970s staple is durable and practical – and will not rot or go mouldy. Made from the outer bark of the cork oak, it is also easily sustainable, since the bark can be harvested every eight to ten years without damaging the tree. Cork wall tiles are available in a variety of thicknesses, grades and dimensions. Warm, springy and resilient, cork comes in a selection of colours spanning natural shades of caramel and honey through to darker, more sombre tones. Ideal in minimalist interiors, cork tiles introduce a textural element while still maintaining a basically neutral feel.

Wood tiles also offer a wide range of choice in terms of grain and colour. For a naturalistic look, mix different woods – from pale maple to dark walnut – to create an interesting chequerboard effect.

POLYSTYRENE

One of the fastest and most cost-effective methods of creating an original wall decoration is to customize your own designs using polystyrene ceiling tiles. For a modern graphic effect, paint tiles in a colour of your choice and stick them on to walls in a grid pattern. Alternatively, compose a three-dimensional display by pinning on plastic flowers, flip-flops or rubber ducks for a quirky installation that is part conceptual art, part wallcovering.

OPPOSITE Cork wall tiles combine with a fake-grass carpet and a wood table for a naturalistic effect that looks both spontaneous and stylish.

RIGHT A variety of tiles, each faced with a different wood veneer, create a check-effect wallcovering that looks warm and inviting.

'Those who do not want to imitate anything, produce nothing.'
SALVADOR DALI

Panels stylish cladding

WOOD

Appreciated as much for its insulating properties as for its decorative merits, wood panelling has been used to clad walls since the Middle Ages. During the seventeenth and eighteenth centuries when European timber stocks were plentiful and cheap, wood panelling, particularly pine, was the most common wall finish in domestic interiors, providing an effective means of insulation against cold stone or brick walls. Wood was either grained to resemble the hardwoods used for panelling in the most expensive interiors or, more commonly, painted. These days wood panelling is likely to celebrate the warm colours and linear grain of wood in its natural state. Knotty pine – either planked or panelled – is a ubiquitous finish in American homes, while the rich warm colour and simple appearance of redwood, another popular timber, gives an unpretentious rustic quality to Stateside interiors.

Even if your home does not need any extra insulation, the psychological effect of wood-clad walls is very powerful, evoking feelings of warmth, comfort and security. Horizontal planks re-create the cosy ambience of a log cabin, while plain plywood strips damp down acoustics and bestow a reassuring feeling of enclosure. This sensation of 'wrapping' interiors is particularly valid in bedrooms and living areas, where the creation of a relaxed and comforting atmosphere is of prime importance.

Match-boarding, or tongue-and-groove as it is known today, was often used in the eighteenth and nineteenth centuries, especially in rustic interiors where a relaxed look predominated. Consisting of plain planks of softwood framed by posts, match-boarding was a practical way of covering walls and was frequently used for dados as an effective way to resist wear and tear. In contemporary interiors textural tongue-and-groove offers a fast and stylish way of 'naturalizing' your space, while the linearity

of textured planks has a wonderfully calming effect. Widely available in kit form, tongue-and-groove is increasingly emerging from the bathroom, where it has long been used to box in bathtubs and hide unattractive pipework, and is now just as likely to clad the walls in bedrooms, kitchens and living areas.

A key advantage of tongue-and-groove is its ability to cover up a multitude of horrors – from unattractive wallpaper to unsightly damp patches. Painted tongue-and-groove can also yield a variety of different looks: for example, dark-coloured boards give a smart sombre feel; bright colours such as orange or pink create an instantly hip ambience; white has a pure Zen simplicity; and multicoloured boards recall the gaiety and charm of simple beach huts. Alternatively, lime tongue-and-groove boards or leave them raw to give a reassuring rustic feel.

Cladding walls with bamboo is another decorating device that is being increasingly used in contemporary homes. A woody grass, rather than a true wood, bamboo is currently finding favour as an environmentally acceptable alternative to endangered hardwoods. The gently rippled appearance of walls clad in panels of bamboo provides the perfect backdrop for Eastern-style furnishings such as shoji screens, paper lamps and glossy lacquer.

Yet another type of wood panelling is plywood sheet, which emphasizes a plane of wall in the same way that a splash of brightly coloured paint does. The contrast between plaster and wood works especially well when used to define areas of activity within an open-plan space – on a wall flanking an eating area, for example, or to divide a living/working area. Plywood sheets that have been screen-printed – a zany new design concept – offer a modern alternative to plainer styles, and look fabulous when used to create a kind of extended bedhead.

ABOVE Tongue-and-groove boards are an effective way of introducing texture into interiors.

OPPOSITE Contemporary wood-panelled walls glory in the warm colours and linear grain of wood in its natural state.

METAL, MIRROR AND GLASS

Capable of appearing utilitarian and basic, or sleek and sophisticated, metal wall panels are a great way to imbue interiors with a raw energy as well as a cool contemporary feel. Sharp and defiantly hard-edged, the metal aesthetic is a simple treatment that ages well, although it should be remembered that a little goes a long way: interiors entirely clad in metal can be harsh, noisy and unforgiving.

The best thing about metal wallcoverings is the wealth of finishes available, enabling the creation of countless different looks. For example, polished metal strikes a bright functional note, its shiny surface adding sparkle and reflectivity as well as enhancing light options. Most commonly used in kitchens, where its pristine appearance reinforces an impression of efficiency and professionalism, polished metal can seem a little brash when new, but acquires a pleasingly mottled patina over time, which helps to soften the initial effect.

Other varieties of metal cladding include brushed stainless steel, which has a soft, shimmery appearance. Sold plain or with gridded or ridged relief patterns, it has a graceful fluidity that is particularly suited to rooms washed with lots of natural light. Aluminium cladding that is light and rust-resistant is another option if you want to create an industrial look. Available in a brushed finish or with relief dots in varying sizes, aluminium sheeting can be used as a ceiling cover to create a sleek, urban effect.

For a modern edgy look, perforated metal plate is ideal; combine it with furnishings in leather, chrome and glass to give an urbane macho appearance. Alternatively, clad walls with corrugated metal. Widely used as siding or roofing in prefabricated sheds and buildings, it has an unmistakable rippled appearance that is simple and unpretentious, yet endows walls with additional depth and texture. Use shiny corrugated aluminium as a modern splashback in an all-metal kitchen – or paint it white if a softer, more fluid effect is desired.

Mirrors, with their multiple reflections and ability to fracture light, are guaranteed to imbue your living space with a glinty depth and drama. Hang a single floor-to-ceiling reflective panel in an unexpected place to surprise the eye, or utilize the slightly foxed surface of vintage glass to create a sense of intrigue and timelessness.

Large expanses of clear glass can be used to harness light in contemporary interiors and give a cool, clean feel. Coloured-glass laminate – either transparent or opaque – will give additional interest, while glass that has been etched or sandblasted provides yet another option.

'Everything depends on how we use a material, not on the material itself.'

MIES VAN DER ROHE

HERE More like an art installation than a wallcovering, these glass panels emphasize the curve of the wall without compromising the minimalist décor.

PLASTIC

Far from appearing tacky, plastic wallcoverings are, actually, a relatively inexpensive way to give interiors a stylish spin. Classic plastics by designers such as Verner Panton routinely exceed their estimates at auction, and include his injection-moulded plastic wall panels, which he designed in the 1970s. Manufactured in a variety of brilliant colours including purple, scarlet, gold and silver, they have a glossy space-age appearance and are great for injecting interiors with a seriously retro vibe. Coloured Perspex panels also work well in modern spaces: use them to glam up one wall of an all-white room or to make a funky bedhead. Alternatively, coloured Perspex tiles that have been backlit provide cheerful illumination, while corrugated-plastic panels painted to imitate brushed aluminium offer a lighter and warmer version of the real thing.

Rubber is another natural material that is fast becoming de rigueur in contemporary interiors. Most often associated with flooring, it also makes a trendy wallcovering. Practical, warm and a good sound insulator, rubber originally made its way into our homes during the hi-tech period of the late 1970s when industrial fittings were all the rage. Today its robust matt finish is once again being called into play. Available in a vast range of colours and finishes, rubber is usually sold in tile form, facilitating the creation of funky chequerboard designs. Usually associated with kitchens and bathrooms, rubber can also be used to clad the walls of living rooms and play areas, while its anti-static properties make it ideal for technology-heavy home offices.

OPPOSITE Walls clad in plastic tiles give interiors a robust, irreverent feel, especially when used in candy colours.

ABOVE Plastic cobbles on a wall provide a kitsch aesthetic and help to introduce a pleasing textural element.

Techniques

Wallpaper

PRACTICAL CONSIDERATIONS

All rolls of wallcoverings should have suitability or 'International Performance' symbols printed on the label or on the wallcovering swatch in the book. Check them before you buy to ensure they are suited to the area for which they are intended.

Before papering, prepare the wall to provide a sound base for hanging the paper. Applying expanded-polystyrene sheeting before the wallcovering will reduce condensation in humid areas such as kitchens and bathrooms. Lining with a thick paper is necessary to give heavy or expensive wallcoverings a good base, and can help smooth over imperfections that lightweight papers and foil coverings will accentuate.

HANGING PAPER

CHECKLIST

- Retractable measure
- Spirit level, plumbline and pencil
- Wallpaper of your choice
- Paper-hanging table
- Wallpaper scissors and trimming knife
- Wallpaper adhesive*
- Plastic bowl or bucket for mixing paste
- Wallpaper brush
- Stepladder
- Smoothing brush
- Seam roller
- Cellulose sponge
- * Always use the adhesive recommended by the manufacturer

TIP

Work out how much wallpaper you will need before buying. Check that all rolls have the same batch number and buy slightly more than required, as another batch can look conspicuously different.

1 Start by determining the room's focal point, which is usually the wall opposite the door. That is where any pattern should be centred. Find the centrepoint of the wall and, using the spirit level, pencil a vertical line through it from top to bottom of the wall.

2 Working outwards from the centred line and towards the corners, measure the width of the paper and mark where each subsequent strip of paper will need to be hung, using the spirit level for accuracy.

3 For simple floor-to-ceiling lengths, measure off a strip allowing 15 cm (6 in) overhang at the top and bottom for trimming to size once the paper is in situ. Make sure the pattern is central on the first length, as this will be your guide for judging the pattern repeat on subsequent drops.

4 When you have cut your first strip, lay it face down on the table and apply the paste evenly, ensuring the edges are coated, too. Wallpaper needs 'booking' because this lets the paste penetrate it and prevents it from drying out. It also allows the strip to relax, as it can stretch when damp. Fold the ends of the strip into the middle so the pasted sides touch. Do not press into folds. Fold in half again then roll the strip loosely from one end to the other.

5 The manufacturer's guidelines for booking should be read before hanging. Then take the paper up the ladder with you and unroll it, undo the first fold and peel back to free the top end. Don't unravel too much, as long strips can be tricky to manoeuvre. Lift into position, lining up the strip with the vertical line and leaving the overhang at the top and bottom for trimming.

6 Working upwards and outwards, smooth out air bubbles or wrinkles with the soft dry smoothing brush. Place 2–3 more strips, making sure the pattern matches and butting the edges for a neat finish. A seam roller will ensure good adhesion, but do not press too hard as it will make a noticeable indentation. Crease along the paper where the wall meets the skirting or ceiling, then trim along the creases. Remove any adhesive on the surface with a damp sponge.

DEALING WITH CORNERS

Few walls meet at the corners in a true right angle. To deal with inside corners, measure from the last vertical guideline at the bottom, middle and top into the corner, adding 2 cm (¾ in) for an overlap. Paste the wallpaper and cut to the measurements, ensuring the pattern matches. Butt to the plumbline and smooth the cut edge into the corner.

Measure the waste strip of paper and mark out from the corner on to the adjoining wall. Use the spirit level to draw a vertical line through the

LEFT Patterned panels propped up against the wall provide an alternative to wall-to-wall coverage.

FAR LEFT Lining walls with a thick paper will give a good base for expensive or heavy wallcoverings.

PAPERING AROUND SOCKETS AND SWITCHES

Always turn the power off first. Remove the coverplate. Hang the paper up and lightly press it around the switch or socket casing. Use the trimming knife to make two diagonal cuts forming an 'X' across the casing. Cut away the excess paper covering the casing. Use a dry cloth to wipe off any adhesive and refit the coverplate.

PHOTO-WALL
CHECKLIST

· Chisel and mallet
· Wallpaper size
· Printed photo-wall or picture-mural sheets
· Wallpaper adhesive*
· Plastic bowl or bucket for mixing paste
· Spirit level, measure and pencil
· Wallpaper brush
· Trimming knife
* Use the adhesive recommended by the photo-wall manufacturer

1 Prepare the wall surface as you would for paint (see page 146). Strip off old wallpaper and treat any damp patches or stains with a stain-blocking or antidamp paint to prevent them damaging the new image.

2 Remove the skirting board (baseboard), levering it away from the wall with the chisel and mallet. Size the wall first so the adhesive does not soak into the wall before it has secured the panels.

3 Depending on whether you are having a full photo-wall of 8 panels, a halfwall of 4 panels or a widescape design of 4 panels, you will need to spread the picture on the floor or over a table.

4 Make the wallpaper paste and leave for 15–20 minutes to work. To ensure the design is centred on the wall, use the spirit level and a pencil to draw a horizontal line across the wall, halfway between the floor and ceiling.

5 Working in the order in which the sheets will have been numbered, take sheet one and apply the paste to the back, brushing diagonally across from bottom left. Lift the sheet into position, using the line on the wall as your guide.

6 Repeat for the remaining pieces, following the manufacturer's guidelines. Leave an overlap of 3 mm (⅛ in) between the top and bottom sections for a neat finish. Trim away the excess and let dry before replacing the skirting board (baseboard).

HANGING PAPER BANNERS
CHECKLIST

· Paper(s)
· 6 mm (¼ in) dowelling
· Clear adhesive
· Staple gun and scissors
· 20 mm (¾ in) softwood 'D' batten (strip)
· Nylon cord
· Picture hook/nail and hammer

1 Spread the paper banner face-down on a flat surface. Cut the dowelling to the width of the paper's top edge, allowing a 1 cm (½ in) overhang on each side to attach the cord. Squeeze a fine line of adhesive along the top edge of the paper and place the dowelling on it.

2 Roll the paper once around the dowelling, fix with staples every 15 cm (6 in) and allow to dry. Repeat, using the softwood batten at the bottom.

3 Cut a length of cord and tie each end to the dowelling overhang. Hold the banner up to the wall and mark the position for the picture hook. Tap in the hook and hang up the banner.

---

mark. Hang the waste strip with the straight edge true to the vertical line and the cut edge overlapping the corner. Smooth the paper and trim top and bottom.

PAPERING AROUND DOORS AND WINDOWS

Measure and cut a full-length strip of wallpaper as before. Paste, then position the paper loosely right over the door or window, making sure the strip accurately matches the previous one. Hold the strip securely and make a diagonal cut from the edge of the strip across the door or window to the outer corner of the frame where it meets the wall. For windows, make a second diagonal cut down to the bottom corner.

Use the blunt edge of the scissors to press the paper into the crease between the windowframe and wall and across the top of the frame. Check the paper is still aligned to the previous strip. A third crease will need to be made along the bottom of windows. Trim off the excess paper and smooth the paper to fit. Repeat to cover the opposite side of the window or door.

Paint

PRACTICAL CONSIDERATIONS

Nothing will transform a room more speedily or inexpensively than a coat of fresh paint. But before you lift a paint brush, the walls will need to be prepared to ensure the paintwork not only looks good, but lasts well, too. Even rough- and rustic-textured finishes need to be applied to a sound base to prevent them from appearing simply neglected.

Remember that more elaborate paint effects need time to perfect – particularly when covering a large wall surface. Avoiding patchiness is the biggest problem, especially where a new batch of paint has to be mixed at the halfway stage, or when you simply get tired. Practise the paint effect on large pieces of hardboard until you are satisfied that you can achieve a consistent result.

SAFETY

Always work in a well-ventilated room and wear a protective mask to avoid inhaling paint fumes.

PREPARING SURFACES

CHECKLIST

- Decorating sheets
- Bucket
- Sugar soap or other strong detergent
- White spirit (turpentine)
- Cotton cloths
- Cellulose sponge
- General-purpose filler paste
- Filling (putty) knife
- Sanding block
- Low-tack masking tape

1 Move smaller items of furniture out of the room before covering the floors, sofas and remaining furniture with the decorating sheets. Make up the sugar-soap or detergent solution following the manufacturer's guidelines.

2 Previously painted walls and woodwork need to be washed down thoroughly first. To prevent streaks, work from the bottom of the wall to the top. Remove oily marks by rubbing with a little white spirit (turpentine) on a clean cloth. Sponge the walls with fresh water and wipe off the excess with cloths. Allow the walls to dry.

3 A powdery surface on walls will prevent any new paint from adhering properly so should be treated with a stabilizing solution. Marks caused by smoky atmospheres, rust or grease should be covered with a stain-cover paint to prevent them 'bleeding' through the new paint surface.

4 Use the filling (putty) knife to remove any loose plaster from large cracks and press the filler paste into them to ensure a good bond. Settlement and shrinkage gaps will recur unless a flexible filler is used. This can be applied with a special 'gun' or directly from the tube if fitted with a nozzle. Allow to dry thoroughly before sanding smooth.

5 To prevent paint splats on nearby surfaces, cover the top of skirting boards (baseboards), light switches and the frames of windows and doors with low-tack tape.

BASIC PAINTING

Rollers are excellent for applying paint to large areas. Choose a short-pile sleeve for a smooth finish or a synthetic or wool one for more texture. Rollers between 15 cm (6 in) and 22.5 cm (9 in) long hold less paint than bigger ones, but are lighter and easier to manoeuvre. Always choose good-quality brushes to avoid bristles being shed.

CHECKLIST

- Emulsion (latex) paint
- Paint roller and tray
- 5 cm (2 in) or 7.5 cm (2¾ in) paint brush
- Clean cloths
- Stepladder

TIP

To work out how much paint you will need, calculate the area (width x height – don't worry about windows or doors) in square metres (yards). Then refer to the instructions on the container of paint you want to use to find the average coverage. Most emulsions (latex paints) will cover roughly 15 square metres per litre (45 square yards per gallon), but less on new plaster or textured surfaces.

1 Pour a small amount of paint into the reservoir of the tray. Dip the roller into the paint and run it across the ridged surface until it is coated evenly.

2 Hold the roller firmly against the wall, working in all directions, and use zigzag strokes to achieve an even coverage. Use the paint brush in areas where the roller will not work – wall and ceiling edges, mouldings and around light switches. For a good solid colour, apply two coats of paint, allowing to dry for the recommended time between each coat.

STONEWASHED-DENIM EFFECT

CHECKLIST

- White and dark blue emulsion (latex) paint
- 15 cm (6 in) and 10 cm (4 in) decorating brushes
- Clean cotton cloths
- Stippling brush
- Ruler
- Stencil brush
- Fine artist's brushes
- Artist's acrylic paints in cobalt blue and yellow ochre

1 Cover the wall with a base coat of white emulsion (latex). When it is dry, apply a dilute solution of 2 parts dark blue emulsion (latex) to 1 part water over the entire surface. Before it dries, rub with the cloths to remove excess paint, leaving an all-over shaded effect.

2 Dip the small brush in the dark blue emulsion (latex). Work off the excess paint by rubbing the bristles on to a cloth. In light straight strokes, run the brush down the wall to make faint lines.

3 Repeat the process, working diagonally. Before the paint dries, soften the lines by dabbing with the stippling brush to remove some of the blue paint; this will create the woven texture of denim.

4 To mimic jean seams, run a little white paint along the edge of a ruler then press the ruler on to the wall in straight or random lines. Soften the lines by working along them with a dry brush. Dip the stencil brush in cobalt blue acrylic and dab the bristles over a cloth until almost dry. Work next to the white 'seams' in irregular patches to achieve the characteristic shading.

5 Finish with a series of fine broken stitches, using an artist's brush and yellow ochre acrylic.

PEWTER EFFECT

This works well on lightly textured surfaces where good lighting will create dramatic highlights.

CHECKLIST

- Dove-grey emulsion (latex) paint
- Silver spray paint
- Black water-based paint
- 15 cm (6 in) and 10 cm (4 in) decorating brushes and a thick short-bristled brush
- Clean cloths

1 Paint the wall grey. When dry, spray silver paint across the wall. Do not worry if the effect is uneven, as this gives a more textural look.

2 Thin the black paint with an equal part water to create a colourwash. Apply over the whole wall and work into the surface so that it is transparent in some patches but darker in others, removing some of the black paint as you go.

HERE Painted stripes give a funky linear effect, and are simply and easily achieved using low-tack masking tape.

3 Lightly spray the silver spray paint across the surface in a diagonal direction to create additional silvery highlights. If the paint should spatter, use the dry decorating brush to rub out the paint spots before they dry.

BLACKBOARD PANEL

Thick, matt and durable, blackboard paint can be applied directly on to a wall to cover a large area, or low-tack tape can be used to protect the surrounding wall while treating a smaller section.

However, should you want to paint over a blackboard wall at a later stage, it will need to be sanded down first and may require two or more coats of paint to cover it adequately. Painted hardboard panels, which are fixed to the wall with screws, have the advantage of being easily removed when desired.

CHECKLIST
- Hardboard
- Blackboard paint
- Paint brush
- Drill
- Wall plugs
- Screws
- Hacksaw
- Wood moulding or metallic trim
- Glue gun

1 Ask the supplier to cut the hardboard to size for you. Paint the hardboard face (the smooth surface) with one coat of blackboard paint. Allow to dry thoroughly overnight.

2 Mark the drill holes in the corners of the hardboard and hold firmly in position against the wall. Drill through the board and into the wall, then remove the board and fit the holes with wall plugs. Screw to secure.

3 To tidy the edges, use the hacksaw to cut a wood moulding or metallic strip to fit, then glue in position. Wood mouldings can be finished in a stain or paint colour of your choice before gluing.

GLITTER-FINISH EFFECT

Coloured glitter can be applied in a variety of ways. The simplest is an all-over effect. You will need to choose a paint colour for the wall's base coat, which can be in a matt or satin finish. The glue, although milky in colour, dries clear, allowing the base colour to show and the glitter to sparkle.

CHECKLIST
- Base-paint colour of your choice
- PVA white glue
- Glitter
- Paint brush

1 Paint the walls the colour of your choice (see page 146). Allow to dry thoroughly.

LEFT Glitter paint gives an instantly glamorous sheen; use dark colours for dramatic effect.

ABOVE It is possible to mix and match florals so long as designs are similar in colour, mood and type.

2 In a clean paint can, mix together equal parts of PVA white glue and water and stir in the glitter until it is evenly distributed.

3 Brush the entire wall surface with the glue-and-glitter mixture, stirring the mix regularly to keep the glitter evenly distributed.

VARIATIONS

Use a measure and pencil and low-tack tape to make stripes or squares over the entire wall or a section of wall. Apply the glue-and-glitter mixture within the areas for a geometric pattern.

Create a night-sky effect by first painting the walls a deep navy colour. When the paint is still wet, scatter the glitter randomly for the galaxies. Larger stars can be added when the paint is dry – either by using fragments of artist's foil stuck with PVA white glue or by mixing the glue with glitter and applying it in clusters.

Panelling

PRACTICAL CONSIDERATIONS

As well as enhancing a room's style, panelling can cover uneven walls and unsightly pipework, wiring or ducting. It can also provide additional insulation if polystyrene or thermal sheeting is fitted between the wall and panels. Panelling is designed to be tough, taking the knocks and scuffs that wallpaper won't withstand, which makes it highly useful in heavy-duty areas.

SAFETY

When fitting battens (furring strips), make sure that there are no water pipes or electrical wiring behind the wall.

WAINSCOT PANELLING

CHECKLIST
- Crowbar or chisel and mallet
- Spirit level, measure and pencil
- Drill
- Wall plugs
- Wall battens (furring strips)
- Wood screws and screwdriver
- Wainscot panels or softwood tongue-and-groove
- Lost head nails, panel pins and hammer
- Piece of wood or board for uneven corners
- Internal/external corner-angle moulding
- Wood filler
- Sandpaper
- Dado rail
- Cover strip
- Paint or stain finish

1 If you intend to reuse the existing skirting (baseboard), carefully lever it away from the wall with a crowbar or chisel. On long runs, place a block of wood behind the skirting (baseboard) to hold it away from the wall while reinserting the crowbar or chisel. Repeat along the wall.

2 Make pencil marks 82 cm (32¼ in) from the floor, along the wall. Use the spirit level for accuracy. Drill holes at regular intervals along the line and fit with wall plugs. Drill corresponding holes in a batten (strip) and screw it to the wall.

3 Fix a second batten (strip) along the base of the wall and a third centred between the top and bottom battens. Fix the panels or tongue-and-groove to the battens with lost head nails. If the corner of the room is not truly vertical, cut a wedge-shape 'filler' to fit the corner, or insert a piece of wood to pack out the wall.

4 If there are several internal or external corners to work around – such as a chimneybreast or alcove – use corner-angle mouldings that are just glued and pinned in place for a neat finish.

5 Nail the skirting (baseboard) back in place over the panelling. Use a filler to smooth over any gaps, and sandpaper to remove rough joins. Fix the rail or moulding to the top front of the panelling with panel pins or lost head nails. Nail the cover strip to the visible edge of the top batten to hide the cut edges of the panelling.

6 Paint or stain the panelling to finish.

LAMINATED-GLASS PANELLING

Only laminated or safety glass should be used. To meet the standards and building regulations governing the use of glass in the home, discuss its intended application with the supplier before starting a project. Because of the large sheets and specialist fixings needed for floor-to-ceiling partitions, professional installation is essential.

However, small coloured laminated-glass sheets can be wall-mounted as a series of glass panels. For best effect they should stand away from the wall by 2.5 cm (1 in) to allow light to filter between the glass and the wall behind. Ask the supplier to predrill fixing holes.

CHECKLIST
- Laminated/safety-glass panel(s)
- Spirit level, measure and pencil
- Drill
- Wall plugs
- Mirror screws with covers
- Spacer rings

1 Measure the position for each panel, pencilling marks on the wall. Hold each glass panel against the wall and mark the hole positions.

2 Drill the holes and fit with wall plugs. Holding each glass panel securely, slide the mirror screws through and fit with a spacer ring. Lift into position and screw the mirror screws firmly into place. Conceal the screw heads with the covers.

PLEXIGLAS AND ACRYLIC SHEET

Plexiglas can be moulded to create unusual and amoebic forms, adding interest to large blank walls. Acrylic sheets are more widely available and come in a broad range of colours and sizes, the largest standard size being 2.4 m x 1.2 m (8 ft x 4 ft) – above this you will need custom sizes. For fixing these sheets to walls, always follow the manufacturer's recommendations.

STEEL, ALUMINIUM AND COPPER SHEET

Galvanized- and stainless-steel sheets are available through larger DIY and specialist retailers. They can be fixed to walls with a contact adhesive, providing they will not come into contact with direct heat. Alternatively, they can be drilled and screwed to the wall. Aluminium and copper are softer than steel and will bend or scratch, so extra care is needed when handling.

A hacksaw should be fine for cutting small angles, but an angle grinder will give a neater finish. Glue the sheets to MDF or plywood, as they will help prevent knocks from causing dents. Drill through the sheets and screw to the wall.

Fabric

PRACTICAL CONSIDERATIONS

When fine fabrics such as chintz, linen and silk are used for wallcoverings, they can easily stain if they come into contact with water or grease – so use them in light-wear areas such as bedrooms and dining rooms. A fabric protector can be applied to repel liquids; it is relatively simple to do this yourself – test a small area first.

Felt and denim have the advantage of a denser textural weave that can conceal small blemishes. They will not fray and, with no obvious pattern to match, are easier to put up. However, avoid water-based adhesives, as they can penetrate the weave, causing it to stiffen and buckle.

Most wallcoverings with an embossed leather finish or faux-suede pile can be hung in the same way as other fabrics. But if you're going for the real thing, decide whether to stretch and glue the hide to uniformly sized plywood 'tiles' or place it in a random pattern over the wall for a 'crazy paving' look. Either way, make sure you create an even balance of the colour variations and imperfections.

FABRIC WALLCOVERINGS

CHECKLIST
- Lining paper and wallpaper paste (see pages 144–5)
- Paper-hanging table
- Plumbline, measure and pencil
- Adhesive*
- Fabric wallcovering
- Fabric shears
- Felt or rubber roller
- Trimming knife
- PVA white glue
- * Always use the adhesive recommended by the manufacturer. If in doubt, choose a strong fast-tack spray adhesive that is suitable for porous surfaces. Test a sample of the fabric beforehand to check suitability.

1 Any blemish on the walls' surface will show through a fine fabric. Remove any flaking paint and old wallpaper, fill any gaps or cracks and smooth over rough patches. Hang the lining paper horizontally with a good wallpaper paste and allow to dry overnight.

2 The first length of fabric should be centred on the wall opposite the door. Use the plumbline to pencil two vertical lines (the space between should be equal to the width of your fabric). Apply the adhesive to the marked section of the wall, allowing a little to extend over the lines.

3 Cut the first length of fabric, allowing 10 cm (4 in) at the top and bottom to fit. Smooth with the roller, working from the bottom upwards and towards the edges for a smooth finish. Press the fabric into the skirting (baseboard) and ceiling lines, but wait until the adhesive has dried before using the trimming knife to cut away the excess.

4 Working outwards from the centre strip, match the pattern before cutting the next piece of fabric. Apply the adhesive to the wall, making sure none comes into contact with the adjacent section. Overlap the joins and leave to dry before using the knife to cut through both pieces for a perfect join. Glue any loose overlap with PVA white glue.

HANGING FABRIC BANNERS

CHECKLIST
- Fabric
- Sewing kit, including fabric shears
- Wood batten (strip), measuring 3 cm x 2 cm (1¼ in x ¾ in) x width of fabric
- Staple gun
- Self-adhesive touch-and-close tape
- Iron and tea towel
- Spirit level, measure and pencil
- Drill
- Wall plugs
- Countersunk screws and screwdriver

TIP
To prevent puckering along the seams of the fabric, cut off the selvedges if they are tightly woven. Otherwise, snip into them at 5 cm (2 in) intervals to ensure that the banner lies flat and will not curl at the base.

1 Cut a strip of fabric sufficient to wrap around the wooden batten (strip). Use the staple gun to secure the fabric to it. Peel the backing from the hooked side of the touch-and-close tape and place it over the fabric join. Staple through the touch-and-close tape every 10–15 cm (4–6 in) to fix it firmly to the batten.

2 Remove any loose threads and turn the raw edges under, then loosely hand-sew for a neat finish. Use a medium-hot iron to press the fabric smooth, placing a cotton tea towel between the iron and the fabric to prevent damage. Peel the backing from the loop side of the touch-and-close tape and stick to the back top edge of the banner, 1 cm (½ in) from the top. Stitch to secure.

3 Fix the batten (strip) to the wall by first marking its position with a pencil. Use the spirit level to check that it is horizontal. Mark 3 drill holes on the batten – one in the centre and two 5 cm (2 in) from the ends.

4 Hold the batten (strip) along the line pencilled on the wall. Drill through the marked positions on the batten until corresponding dents are made on the wall behind. Remove the batten, then drill the screw holes into the wall at the dented positions and fit with wall plugs.

5 Position the batten (strip) over the drill holes and screw into position to secure to the wall. Press the strip of touch-and-close tape on the back of the banner to the one on the batten. Any creases in the fabric should drop out overnight in a warm room.

FABRIC-COVERED PANELS

CHECKLIST

- Plyboard or insulation board
- Fabric
- Measure
- Fabric shears
- Low-tack masking tape
- Spray adhesive
- PVA white glue
- Drawing pins (thumbtacks)
- Wallboard adhesive or contact glue (optional)

1 Before buying the board, work out the exact size you will need. Many boards come in a standard 2.4 m x 1.2 m (8 ft x 4 ft) size, but they can be cut to your specifications by the supplier, which will make the project easier.

2 Cut the fabric to size, allowing a 10–15 cm (4–6 in) overlap, then place face-down on a flat surface. Hold it taut with a few strips of low-tack tape. Lightly spray the adhesive on one side of the board and place it on top of the fabric. Press firmly to ensure a good contact.

3 Turn the panel over and gently smooth out any ridges or bubbles in the fabric. Wrap the overlap around the edges and secure at the back with glue. Use drawing pins (thumbtacks) to hold the fabric firmly in place until dry.

4 If placing the fabric panel directly on to the wall, use a strong wallboard adhesive or contact glue to secure it in place.

LEFT Fabric wall banners, here in a pleated version, work best in minimalist rooms where their symmetry compounds the ordered calm.

Tiling

PRACTICAL CONSIDERATIONS

Ceramic tiles are the most popular choice for areas such as kitchens and bathrooms that require a more durable surface than paint or wallpaper alone can provide. However, mosaic and stainless-steel tiles are both practical and appropriate for contemporary interiors. Alternatively, cork tiles add texture and warmth to a room and can be painted to suit specific colour schemes.

With the right tools and a little skill, cutting and fitting all these tile types is straightforward, but stone, marble and granite tiles are best left for professional installation.

SAFETY

When snapping, sawing or 'nibbling' ceramic tiles, small chips of glaze tend to fly into the air. Always wear protective goggles and gloves to prevent injury. When fitting battens (furring strips), make sure that there are no water pipes or electrical wiring behind the wall.

CERAMIC TILING

CHECKLIST
- Ceramic tiles
- Tile spacers
- Spirit level, measure and pencil
- Wooden battens (furring strips), hammer and masonry nails (for larger areas)
- Gauge (jury) stick (optional)
- Adhesive
- Adhesive spreader
- Wax pencil
- Tile jig (cutter)
- Tile nibbler (nippers)
- Tile saw
- Waterproof grout and spreader
- Decorator's sponge

GAUGE (JURY) STICK

It is helpful to make a gauge (jury) stick to plot the position of the rows of tiles. Use a 1.5 m (5 ft) long strip of 5 cm x 1.2 cm (2 in x ½ in) softwood. Place it on a table and lay tiles along its length (use spacers unless they are to be close-butted). Mark the position of each tile clearly and use the stick to check regularly that the tiles are being laid correctly.

BEFORE STARTING

If the tiled area is to incorporate a design, plan it first on graph paper so the pattern is centred. Remove all fixtures and make sure the surface is sound and dry. Although it is possible to tile over existing tiles, the resulting thickness can encroach on basins (sinks), baths and windowsills. If this looks likely, use a chisel and hammer to remove them, making sure the surrounding surfaces are protected from debris with decorator's sheets.

1 When tiling a straight run, check that the adjacent surface (such as the countertop or floor) is level. If it is slightly out, nail a batten (wood strip) one tile height from the counter or floor using a spirit level to ensure it is truly horizontal. A vertical batten should be nailed to one side of the area so it is possible to start with whole tiles.

2 Use the spreader to apply the adhesive; allow enough for around 10–12 tiles at one go. Make sure the first tile fits well into the right angle formed by the battens (strips). Continue to attach the tiles, using spacers as required and ensuring that the tips touch the wall surface to make even grooves. Check each row as you proceed to see that it is level.

3 To cut a tile, mark the cutting line with a wax pencil on the glazed side. Run the wheel of the tile jig (cutter) firmly along the line, then push down the handle to snap the tile. When cutting awkward angles to fit around pipes or mouldings,

make a paper template and then transfer it on to the tile. Score around the shape, then in a crisscross pattern on the surplus area. Use the nibbler to break away the excess gradually.

Curves can also be cut with a tungsten-carbide rod saw. Where a pipe will need to go through the centre of a tile, cut the tile in half then nibble away the centre and rejoin the two halves around the pipe. If using tile trim to neaten edges, fit it before the tiles are butted up to it.

4 When the tiling is complete, start on the grouting. Working over a manageable area – roughly a square metre (yard) – at a time, spread sufficient grout over the tiles to fill the gaps. Scrape off the excess grout, then sponge off any residue on the surface of the tiles. To neaten the grout lines between tiles, run the blunt end of a pencil along them. When the grout is dry, buff the tiles' surface with a soft lint-free cloth.

TIPS

Do not worry if you are unable to finish large areas in one go. Leaving the adhesive to dry overnight will help prevent slippage and give following rows of tiles a secure base.

Profile tiles tend to be bulkier and thicker than standard ceramic tiles and it is best to score along any cut lines before trimming to size with a tile saw or angle grinder. Narrow tile strips can snap easily; to avoid this happening, place them on a firm surface and secure either side of the cut line with adhesive tape.

When drilling into tiles to secure fixtures, place clear adhesive tape over areas to be drilled to prevent the drill bit from slipping.

CORK

With their natural texture, cork tiles instantly add interest to walls. They are easily cut to fit with a heavy-duty trimming knife and a cutting board or old surface to cut on. Make sure that the wall is free from loose paint and wallpaper beforehand, and always use a proprietary rubber-based cork-tile adhesive to secure the tiles.

A horizontal guide batten (wood strip) should be nailed to the base of the wall, and a plumbline used to mark a vertical line in the centre of the wall to work out from in both directions.

MIRROR

The glass surface as well as the silvering on the back of mirror tiles can be damaged by inexperienced handling. To prevent expensive mistakes, take tiles that require precision cutting to a glass retailer, with your templates, so they can be cut with minimum wastage. Remember that if the wall is at all uneven, the tiles will throw a distorted image, so it is important to check for lumps and level out any you find before commencing tiling.

MOSAIC

Opting for individual mosaic chips opens up the possibility of creating totally unique designs in the colours of your choice. Plan the design on graph paper beforehand, or lay out the mosaic pattern on a flat surface so that it can be accurately applied to the wall as you work. Many mosaic tiles are supplied in sheet form

with a mesh backing that can be cut easily to fit internal and external corners as well as around pipework and mouldings. Sheets of mosaic tiles fixed to paper can be laid directly on fresh tile adhesive. Moistening the paper allows it to be peeled away, leaving the tiles uniformly spaced.

Make a small carpet-covered board, place it pile-side down against the tiles and tap lightly with a mallet to make sure they bed down well. Use a waterproof and stain-resistant grout to help keep the mosaic looking clean.

STAINLESS STEEL

Expert cutting with a diamond-tip angle grinder is required for stainless-steel tiles. Hire one for the job or ask your supplier to cut the tiles once you have worked out the cut lines and marked them with a permanent marker or wax pencil. Rough-cut edges should be smoothed with a metal file.

STONE AND BRICK TILING

During the 1960s and 1970s thin stone and brick masonry tiles became ubiquitous as focal-point chimneybreasts in homes. Now the look is raw and architectural, and stone and brick can work as a ground for abstract wall art, both in their untreated state or whitewashed.

CHECKLIST

- Stone or brick tiles
- Preformed corner tiles
- Spirit level, measure and pencil
- Gauge (jury) stick
- Hacksaw (for cutting shapes from tiles to fit around pipes, as necessary)
- Tile adhesive
- Notched spreader
- Ready-mixed mortar and spreader
- Bristle brush

1 Leaving joint spaces between each tile, plot the tile courses horizontally and vertically, using a gauge (jury) stick with joint spaces marked (see page 152).

2 Plot your spacing so that ideally you have one course of whole bricks followed by one containing half tiles at each end. Start laying the first course by fixing three preformed corner tiles at the external corners to look like authentic brickwork. Use the notched spreader to apply the adhesive to the back of the tile.*

3 Staggering the vertical joints, continue working up from the base of the wall. Every three courses, use the spirit level to check the brick tiles are level at both ends of the wall, and realign if necessary.

4 Leave the tiles overnight before pointing the joints with a ready-mixed mortar. Remove any mortar residue from the surface of the stones or bricks with a bristle brush.

*Always follow the manufacturer's instructions, as some recommend applying the tile adhesive directly to the wall instead.

LEFT AND BELOW Digital imaging has turned traditional tile design on its head. Use kaleidoscopic patterns to jazz up the walls in your kitchen or bathroom.

DIRECTORY

For manufacturers and designers of wallcoverings that appear in the book, please refer to the picture credits (pages 159–60) and the addresses below.

Adelphi Paper Hangings
PO Box 494
The Plains, VA 20198-0494
USA
tel: 540 253 5367
www.adelphipaperhangings.
com

Alma Home
12–14 Greatorex Street
London E1 5NF
England
tel: 020 7377 0762
www.almahome.co.uk

Anna French Ltd
343 Kings Road
London SW3 5ES
England
tel: 020 7351 1126
www.anna-french.demon.co.uk

Baer & Ingram
273 Wandsworth Bridge
  Road
London SW6 2TX
England
tel: 020 7736 6111
mail order: 0137 381 3800
www.baer-ingram.co.uk

Benetton paints
B & Q
Head Office
1 Hampshire Corporate Park
Chandlers Ford
Eastleigh
Hampshire SO53 3YY
England
tel: 0845 222 1000
www.diy.com

Bradbury & Bradbury
Benicia Arsenal
940 Tyler Street
Benicia, CA 94510
USA
tel: 707 746 1900
www.bradbury.com

Brunschwig & Fils
979 Third Avenue
12th Floor
New York, NY 10022-1234
USA
tel: 212 838 7878
www.brunschwig.com

also at:
10 The Chambers
Chelsea Harbour Drive
London SW10 0XF
England
tel: 020 7351 5797

Cath Kidston
8 Elystan Street
London SW3 3NS
England
tel: 020 7584 3232
mail order: 020 7229 8000
www.cathkidston.co.uk

Claire O'Hea
Studio 33
Great Western Studios
Great Western Road
London W9 3NY
England
tel: 020 8964 3664
coh@dircon.co.uk

Clarence House
211 East 58th Street
New York, NY 10022
USA
tel: 212 752 2890
www.clarencehouse.
  com

also at:
3/10 Chelsea Harbour
  Design Centre
London SW10 0XE
England
tel: 020 7351 1200

Cole & Son Wallpapers
G10 Chelsea Harbour
  Design Centre
London SW10 0XE
England
tel: 020 7376 4628
www.cole-and-son.com

Colefax & Fowler
110 Fulham Road
London SW3 6RL
England
tel: 020 7244 7427
www.iida.co.uk

Colourlink Creative
41–7 Old Street
London EC1 9HX
England
tel: 020 7549 8231
www.colourlinkcreative.
  co.uk

De Gournay Ltd
112 Old Church Street
London SW3 6EP
England
tel: 020 7823 7316
www.degournay.com

Designers Guild
275–7 Kings Road
London SW3 5EN
England
tel: 020 7243 7300
www.designersguild.com

E W Moore
39 Plaishet Grove
London E6 1AD
England
tel: 020 8471 9392
www.wallpapers.org.uk

Eley Kishimoto
Places & Spaces
30 Old Town
London SW4 0LB
England
tel: 020 7498 0998

Ella Doran Ltd
Unit H, Ground Floor South
95–7 Redchurch Street
London E2 7DJ
England
tel: 020 7613 0782
mail order: 020 7729 8378
www.elladoran.co.uk

F Schumacher & Co
79 Madison Avenue
New York, NY 10016
USA
tel: 212 213 7900
www.fschumacher.com

Fornasetti
Via Manzoni, 45
20121 Milano
Italy
tel: 02659 23 41
www.fornasetti.com

Happell
256 High Street
Glasgow G4 0QT
Scotland
tel: 0141 552 7723
www.happell.co.uk

J R Burrows
PO Box 522
Rockland, MA 02370
USA
tel: 800 347 1795
www.burrows.com

Jane Churchill
151 Sloane Street
London SW1X 9BZ
England
tel: 020 7730 9847

Jocelyn Warner
19–20 Sunbury Workshops
Hocker Street
London E2 7LF
England
tel: 020 7613 4773
www.jocelynwarner.com

Kate Maestri
2.11 Oxo Tower Wharf
Bargehouse Street
London SE1 9PH
England
tel: 020 7620 0330

Kate Osborn
tel: 020 7727 0949
www.photo-furnishings.
com

Mulberry Home
41–2 New Bond Street
London W1R 2YS
England
tel: 020 7491 3900
www.mulberry-england.
co.uk

Muriel Short Designs Ltd
Hewitts Estate
Elmbridge Road
Surrey GU6 8LW
England
tel: 0148 327 1211
www.murielshort.com

Neisha Crosland
137 Fulham Road
London SW3 6DS
England
tel: 020 7589 4866
www.neishacrosland.com

also at:
16 West 55th Street
Suite 1R
New York, NY 10019
USA
tel: 212 397 8257

Nobilis–Fontan
29 Rue Bonaparte
75006 Paris
France
tel: 1 43 29 21 50
www.nobilis.fr

Also at:
G3 Chelsea Harbour
 Design Centre
London SW10 OXF
England
tel: 020 7351 7878

Nobilis Inc
57A Industrial Road
Berkeley Heights, NJ 07922
USA
tel: 908 464 1177

Ornamenta
3/12 Chelsea Harbour
 Design Centre
London SW10 0XE
England
tel: 020 7352 1824
www.ornamenta.co.uk

Osborne & Little
304–8 Kings Road
London SW3 5UH
England
tel: 020 7352 1456
www.osborneandlittle.
com

Ottilie Stephenson
101 Redchurch Street
London E2 7DG
England
tel: 020 7739 7321

Paint & Paper Library
5 Elystan Street
London SW3 3NT
England
tel: 020 7823 7755
www.paintlibrary.co.uk

Paper Moon
The Paddocks
29 Bragbury Lane
Bragbury End
Hertfordshire SG2 8TJ
England
tel: 0143 821 1770
www.papermoon.co.uk

Pussy Home Boutique
3a Kensington Gardens
Brighton BN1 4AL
England
tel: 0127 360 4861
www.pussyhomeboutique.
co.uk

Sanderson
Sanderson House
Oxford Road
Denham UB9 4DX
England
tel: 0189 583 0000
www.sanderson-uk.com

also at:
Arthur Sanderson & Sons Ltd
Suite 409
979 Third Avenue
New York, NY 10022
USA
tel: 212 319 7220

Scalamandré
300 Trade Zone Drive
Ronkonkoma, NY 11779
USA
tel: 631 467 8800/
 800 932 4361
www.scalamandre.com

also at:
G4 Chelsea Harbour
 Design Centre
London SW10 0XE
England
tel: 020 7739 1869

Secondhand Rose
138 Duane Street
New York, NY 10013
USA
tel: 212 393 9002
www.secondhandrose.com

Sloane Square Tiles
55 Sloane Square
Cliveden Place
London SW1W 8AX
England
tel: 020 7730 4773

Stencil Library
Stocksfield Hall
Stocksfield
Northumberland NE43 7TN
England
tel: 0166 184 4844
www.stencil-library.com

Stone Paper Knife
No.1 Poultry
London EC2R 8JR
England
tel: 020 7643 2241
www.stonepaperknife.com

Tektura Wall Coverings
1 Heron Quays
Docklands
London E14 4JA
England
tel: 020 7536 3300
www.tekturaonline.com

Timney Fowler
388 Kings Road
London SW3 5U2
England
tel: 020 7352 2263
www.timneyfowler.com

Timorous Beasties
7 Craigend Place
Glasgow G13 2UN
Scotland
tel: 0141 959 3331
www.timorousbeasties.com

Tracy Kendall
116 Greyhound Lane
London SW16 5RN
England
tel: 020 8769 0618
tracy@tkendall.fsbusiness.
 co.uk

Turnell & Gigon
M20 Chelsea Garden
 Market
Chelsea Harbour
London SW10 OXE
England
tel: 020 7351 5142

Ulf Moritz
Bergamo
979 Third Avenue
D & D Building
17th Floor
New York, NY 10022
USA
tel: 212 888 3333
www.bergamofabrics.com

also at:
Brian Yates
G27 Chelsea Harbour
 Design Centre
London SW10 OXE
England
tel: 020 7352 0123

Zuber & Cie
5 Boulevard des Filles
 du Calvaire
75003 Paris
France
tel: 1 42 77 95 91

also at:
Zuber Ltd
42 Pimlico Road
London SW1W 8LP
England
tel: 020 7824 8265

Zuber & Co
979 Third Avenue
New York, NY 10022-1234
USA
tel: 212 486 9226

INDEX

Figures in italics indicate captions.

PICTURE CREDITS

Many of the wallcoverings credited here may be obtained from the listed manufacturers and designers, full addresses of which appear in the Directory (pages 154–5).

Endpapers: courtesy Cole & Son, page 1 courtesy Cole & Son, page 2–3 Polly Wreford / Narratives, page 4–5 Teamworks Wallcoverings Inc., page 6–7 Harbour / Eric Thomas / Moda, page 8 Whitworth Art Gallery, page 9 courtesy De Gournay, page 10–11 Crown Wallcoverings UK, page 12–13 Arcaid, page 14 The Victoria & Albert Museum, page 15l William Morris Pomegranate reproduced by Sanderson / Arcaid 15r Candace Wheeler Honeybee / J R Burrows, page 16 Victoria & Albert Museum, page 17tl Promenade / Willy Herman Studio / Whitworth Art Gallery, 17br courtesy Barnaba Fornasetti / Immaginazione Fornasetti, page18 Verner Panton Design (Basel), page19tr Gyro / June Lyons / Whitworth Art Gallery 19bl Hulton Getty Archive, page 20 Sanderson Palladio / Whitworth Art Gallery, page 21r Chris Tubbs, page 22–3 Victoria & Albert Museum, page 24 Sanderson Palladio / Whitworth Art Gallery, page 25tr Victoria & Albert Museum, 25bl Selection E W Moore, page 26tr Victoria & Albert Museum, 26bl Rene Magritte © ADAGP Paris, page 27l © Damien Hirst / Science, 27r © Sarah Lucas / Sadie Coles HQ, page 28 courtesy Graham & Brown, page 29 courtesy Kate Osborn / © Photo Furnishings, page 30–1 Provence / Lucien Day / Victoria & Albert Museum, page 32 Neisha Crosland / Tom Leighton IPC Syndication / Living etc, page 33 Eley Kishimoto / Elle Decoration UK / Neil Mersh / Stephanie Harding, page 34l Ottilie Stephenson, 34r Baer & Ingram, page 35 Ulf Moritz / courtesy Brian Yates, page 36 Ian Nolan, page 37 Turnell & Gigon, 37b Paper Moon, page 38l Elle Decoration UK / PSC Photography, 38r Elle Decoration UK / Damian Russell / Suzanne Stankus, page 39 Zuber, page 40 Elle Decoration UK / Gary Hamill / Finola Inger, page 41 World of Interiors / Tom Mannion, page 42–3 Ulf Moritz / courtesy Brian Yates, page 44l courtesy Hotel Pelirocco Brighton, page 44–5 Deborah Bowness Hooks and Frocks / courtesy Deborah Bowness, page 46l Schumacher, 46r Teamworks Wallcoverings Inc., page 47 Schumacher, page 48 Mauny, page 49 Daniel Farmer IPC Syndication / Living etc, page 50l courtesy Cath Kidston, 50r Chris Tubbs, page 51 courtesy Sanderson, page 52 Elle Decoration UK / Damian Russell / Amanda Smith, page 53 Clarence House, page 54t Timorous Beasties, 54b Jocelyn Warner, page 55 William Morris Willow Bough reproduced by Sanderson / Chris Brooks / © Carlton Books, page 56t Paper Moon, 56b © Ella Doran, page 57 Tracy Kendall, page 58t Nobilis–Fontan, 58m Schumacher, 58b Schumacher, page 59 Elle Decoration UK / Neil Mersh /

Suzanne Stankus, page 60 Chris Brooks / © Carlton Books, page 61l Paper Moon, 61r Schumacher, page 62l Schumacher, 62b Turnell & Gigon, page 63 Elle Decoration UK / Graham Atkins-Hughes / Emma Thomas, page 64 E W Moore, page 65 Anna French, page 66 Timorous Beasties, page 67 Redcover, page 68 Richard Powers, page 69 from top to bottom: Command / Tektura PLC, Muriel Short, Command / Tektura PLC, Schumacher, page 70 Ulf Moritz / courtesy Brian Yates, page 71 Ulf Moritz / courtesy Brian Yates, page 72 Elle Decoration UK / Graham Atkins-Hughes / Emma Thomas, page 73l Maya Romanoff / Tektura PLC, 73m E W Moore, 73r Neisha Crossland, page 74 Elle Decoration UK / Graham Atkins-Hughes / Emma Thomas, page 75t Nobilis–Fontan, 75b Elle Decoration UK / Graham Atkins-Hughes / Emma Thomas, page 76l courtesy Zuber & Cie, page 76–7 courtesy Deborah Bowness, 77br courtesy Stone Paper Knife, page 78 Cath Kidston, page 79tr Paper Moon, 79bl Narratives / Jan Baldwin, page 80–1 Timney Fowler, page 82l Zuber & Cie, 82–3 Damian Russell IPC Syndication / Living etc, page 83 Chris Brooks / © Carlton Books, page 84 Chris Brooks / © Carlton Books, page 85 Interior Archive / Andrew Wood, page 86 World of Interiors / Bill Batten, page 87 World of Interiors / Bill Batten, page 88t Cole & Son / Malabar, 88bl Narratives / Jan Baldwin, 88br Narratives / Jan Baldwin, page 89 Sanderson Palladio / Whitworth Art Gallery, page 90 Sanderson Palladio / Whitworth Art Gallery, page 91t Palladio Sanderson / Whitworth Art Gallery, 91b Palladio Sanderson / Whitworth Art Gallery, page 92 courtesy Cath Kidston, page 93l Stone Paper Knife, 93r E W Moore page 94 courtesy Tracy Kendall, page 95t courtesy David Oliver / Paint Library, 95b courtesy Tracy Kendall, page 96 Interior Archive / Simon Brown, page 97 Ray Main / Mainstream, page 98–9 Judy Phillips / courtesy Colourlink Creative, page 100 © Ella Doran, page 101 Daniel Ward IPC Syndication / Living etc, page 102t courtesy Hotel Pelirocco Brighton, 102b courtesy Ace Hotel Seattle, page 103 Chris Tubbs, page 104 IPC Syndication / Living etc, page 105 courtesy Ace Hotel Seattle, page 106 courtesy Stone Paper Knife, page 107 Benetton / courtesy Modus Publicity, page 109 Benetton / courtesy Modus publicity page 110l Benetton / courtesy Modus publicity, 110r Benetton / courtesy Modus publicity, page 111l Craig Knowles IPC Syndication / Living etc, 111r Benetton / courtesy Modus publicity, page 112 Mel Yates / © Carlton Books, page 113 Craig Knowles IPC Syndication / Living etc, page 114 Craig Knowles IPC Syndication / Living etc, page 115 Verne/Architect, page 116 Verne/Architect, page 117t © Carlton Books, 117b Verne/Architect, page 118 courtesy The Stencil Library, page 119 courtesy The Stencil Library, page 120t Mel Yates / © Carlton Books,120b courtesy Claire O'Hea, page 121 Elle Decoration UK / Minh & Wass, page 122 Johner / Photonica, page 123 Mel Yates / © Carlton Books page 124 Elle Decoration UK / Graham Atkins-Hughes / Emma Thomas, page 125t courtesy Alma Home,

page 125b Elle Decoration UK / Neil Mersh / Suzanne Stankus, page 126 Elle Decoration UK / Graham Atkins-Hughes / Emma Thomas, page 127 Elle Decoration UK / Graham Atkins-Hughes / Emma Thomas, page 128 courtesy Dominic Crimson / Stone Paper Knife, page 129 courtesy Stone Paper Knife, page 130 courtesy Happell, page 131 courtesy Stone Paper Knife, page 132 Elle Decoration UK / Graham Atkins-Hughes / Emma Thomas, page 133 Elle Decoration UK / Graham Atkins-Hughes / Emma Thomas, page 134 Elle Decoration UK / Graham Atkins-Hughes / Emma Thomas, page 135 Elle Decoration UK / Graham Atkins-Hughes / Emma Thomas, page 136 Elle Decoration UK / Damian Russell / Kristin Perers, page 137 courtesy Cath Kidston, page 138–9 courtesy Kate Maestri, page 140 Elle Decoration UK / Graham Atkins-Hughes / Emma Thomas, page 141 Elle Decoration UK / Graham Atkins-Hughes / Emma Thomas, page 142–3 Vacance / John Line & Sons / Moda, page 144 Laurinda Spear / courtesy Wolf-Gordon Inc., page 145 Simon Brown / Interior Archive, page 147 © Carlton Books, page 148t © Carlton Books, 148b © Carlton Books, 151 Elle Decoration UK / Alex Sarginson / Amanda Smith page 152 courtesy Stone Paper Knife, page 153 courtesy Stone Paper Knife, page 154 Schumacher, page 157 Kate Osborn / © Photo Furnishings page 160 Frivolite / Mary Storr / Moda

Every effort has been made to acknowledge correctly and contact the source and/or copyright holder of each picture and Carlton Books Limited apologizes for any unintentional errors or omissions which will be corrected in future editions of this book.

ACKNOWLEDGEMENTS

Special thanks to:

Rena and Patrick at Cole & Son, Georgia at Sanderson, Carol at Paper Moon, Christine and Penny at the Whitworth Art Gallery Manchester, Elaine and Natalie at the Museum of Domestic Design and Architecture, Andrew at Elle Decoration, Dominic and Tony at Stone Paper Knife, Ella Doran, Zuber & Cie, Alistair and Paul at Timorous Beasties, Sian at Science, Claire O'Hea, Jocelyn Warner, Chris Brooks, Chris Tubbs, Colourlink Creative, De Gournay, Jane at Hotel Pelirocco Brighton, Doug at Ace Hotel Seattle, Kate Osborn, Deborah Bowness, Rachel at The Stencil Library, Tracy Kendall, Dean Happell, The British Council.

The author would like to thank everyone at Carlton Books Limited for all their hard work: Elena Goodinson, Zia Mattocks, Megan Smith.